# Community Server Quickly

A Concise and Practical Guide to Installation,
Administration, and Customization

**Anand Narayanaswamy**

BIRMINGHAM - MUMBAI

# Community Server Quickly

Copyright © 2006 Packt Publishing

First published: November 2006

Production Reference: 1131106

Published by Packt Publishing Ltd.
32 Lincoln Road
Olton
Birmingham, B27 6PA, UK.

ISBN 1-84719-087-1

www.packtpub.com

Cover Image by www.visionwt.com

# Credits

**Author**

Anand Narayanaswamy

**Reviewers**

David Stokes

Rob Howard

**Development Editor**

Douglas Paterson

**Assistant Development Editor**

Nikhil Bangera

**Technical Editors**

Rashmi Phadnis

Viraj Joshi

**Editorial Manager**

Dipali Chittar

**Project Manager**

Patricia Weir

**Indexer**

Bhushan Pangaonkar

**Proofreader**

Chris Smith

**Layouts and Illustrations**

Shantanu Zagade

**Cover Designer**

Shantanu Zagade

# Foreword

We've come a long way from the vision of building a Community Platform. While we are all thrilled with the success the product has had, we are not nearly satisfied and have many more plans for the platform. In fact, we at Telligent believe we have created an entirely unique and new type of solution: a "Community Management System", although the acronym CMS is already taken!

Communities are becoming an increasingly important tool for organizations to use to support their products and initiatives. Communities help you understand and connect to people, such as Microsoft's use of forums.xbox.com as a community for supporting the millions of Xbox gamers. Communities allow you to participate in discussions about your company, people, and products such as Dell's Direct2Dell.com blog. Communities also enable you to create vital tools for talking to customers without spending money on marketing campaigns.

Community Server is the platform that enables all of these scenarios and this book will help introduce you to Community Server and impart the knowledge you need to build a community solution.

In this book, Anand Narayanaswamy will walk you through all of the various capabilities of Community Server, such as how blogs, forums, photo galleries, and file sharing can be used. He will also impart to you some tips & tricks for configuring your Community Server application. More importantly, this book will serve as a handy guide if you are implementing Community Server for your organization.

As I write this foreword our development team is hard at work on version 3.0 of Community Server. The goal for Community Server 3.0 is to greatly simplify the themes engine and to ensure that anyone can make changes to the user experience using simple What You See Is What You Get editors without any knowledge of ASP. NET, CSS, or HTML. At the same time we will not compromise on the platform and Community Server will continue to be a reference software solution that demonstrates best practices for writing software on Microsoft's .NET platform.

With that I present to you this book and hope to see you online at www. communityserver.org.

Thank you,

Rob Howard
Chief Executive Officer
Telligent Systems

# About the Author

**Anand Narayanaswamy** works as an independent consultant and runs NetAns Technologies (`http://www.netans.com`), which provides web hosting services and is based in Trivandrum, Kerala State, India. He is a Microsoft Most Valuable Professional (MVP) in Visual C#. He works as the full time Technical Editor lead for *ASPAlliance.com* (`http://aspalliance.com/author.aspx?uId=38403`) and is also a member of the *ASPAlliance.com* Advisory Board.

He regularly contributes articles, and book and product reviews to *ASPAlliance.com*, *C-Sharpcorner.com*, *Developer.com*, *Codeguru.com*, *Microsoft Academic Alliance*, *asp.netPRO* print magazine, and *asp.netNOW* online magazine.

Anand has worked as a Technical Editor for several popular publishers such as Sams, Addison-Wesley Professional, Wrox, and Manning. His technical editing skills helped the authors of *Sams Teach Yourself the C# Language in 21 Days*, *Core C# and .NET*, *Professional ADO.NET 2*, and *ASP.NET 2.0 Web Parts in Action* to fine tune the content. He has also contributed articles for Microsoft Knowledge Base and delivered podcast shows for *Aspnetpodcast.com*. He is a moderator for Windows MarketPlace Newsgroups.

Anand also runs LearnXpress.com, Dotnetalbum.com, CsharpFAQ.com, Computerbookreviews.org, and DigitalGadget.Info. LearnXpress.com is a featured site at MSDN's Visual C# .NET communities section.

Anand has so far won several prizes at Community-Credit.com and has been featured as "All Time" contributor at the site. He is one of the founders of Trivandrum Microsoft Usergroup. He regularly blogs under the banner "I Type What I Feel" at `http://msmvps.com/anandn` and maintains a personal website at `http://www.visualanand.net/`.

# Acknowledgements

First, I would like to thank my parents for their excellent support and encouragement. I am thankful to my brother for all his help and motivation that made my work better, and I am really proud of him.

I am greatly indebted to Douglas Paterson, Development Editor at Packt Publishing, for accepting my proposal and also for his support from the beginning. He provided valuable advice at every stage through emails that encouraged me a lot. He managed things to ensure that I am not overloaded with work.

My sincere thanks to Rob Howard, Chief Executive Officer, Telligent Systems for his great help right from the beginning despite his busy schedule, by answering several questions very quickly and also for providing a nice Foreword for my book. Rob offered all kind of assistance when I proposed the project to him, and his comments and suggestions as a Technical Reviewer helped me a lot. I am also thankful to David Stokes for his help in reviewing the final set of chapters.

I am thankful to Alex Homer for all his help and support. He quickly replied to my queries, which certainly helped me to complete the project on schedule. I am also thankful to Scott Watermasysk, Jason Alexander, and Donnie Condor for their help and assistance.

I am very much thankful to Nikhil Bangera, Rashmi Phadnis, and Viraj Joshi for nicely editing the content and pinpointing several hidden mistakes in certain chapters. Though I had to work more, I feel that the quality of the book has greatly improved after I incorporated their comments and suggestions into the final drafts. I am thankful to Patricia Weir and the entire staff at Packt Publishing who worked behind this book.

I am thankful to Abhishek Kant, Community Program Manager, Microsoft India for recognizing my talent and expertise. He also provided excellent support whenever I approached him with questions. I am also thankful to Steven A Smith, President, ASPAlliance LLC and Michelle Smith, Vice President, ASPAlliance LLC for their encouragement, help and support.

# About the Reviewers

**Rob Howard** has the privilege of running Telligent (`http://www.telligent.com`) and working with a phenomenal team of talented individuals to build software that helps people share information. Community Server is the first product built by Telligent. Every day Community Server helps people quickly and easily build web communities. Rob's blog is `http://weblogs.asp.net/rhoward` and his email address is `rhoward@telligent.com`.

**Dave Stokes** is a Community Server MVP and has over 20 years experience working with Microsoft products. He has worked for many of the world's leading IT companies in Europe and the United States of America, specializing in Infrastructure Design and Management, and currently spends much of his time packaging applications using Microsoft's Installer Technology. He has been using Community Server since version 1.0. He can be contacted at `dave@davestokes.net`.

# Table of Contents

# Preface

Community Server is an award-winning solution for setting up online communities. It includes a suite of integrated applications, which includes blogs, discussion forums, photo and file galleries, reader, and roller, which together can help you create your community presence. Community Server is the trusted solution for many organizations including Microsoft, Dell, Conde Nast, Match.com, and others. You can learn more about Community Server, and see it in action, at `http://www.communityserver.org`.

Written in a clear and concise manner, this book will guide you through the installation, administration, customization, and deployment of a Community Server solution. With the help of this book you will be able to start using your Community Server site within minutes of its installation. The book kicks off with a brief overview about the evolution of Community Server, its various editions, and installation procedures, and then delves deep into the creation and management of its integrated applications.

The later chapters of the book explore the different ways you can customize your Community Server site along with comprehensive coverage of add-ons and modules. You will also learn how to manage your Community Server license and other related settings.

## What This Book Covers

The Community Server platform is introduced in *Chapter 1* and we look into the evolution of Community Server and various applications available with it. Keeping in mind the nature of tasks that lie ahead, this chapter also discusses various editions and licensing options that will help you to choose the right Community Server platform for your use. Finally it outlines some of the key features of the upcoming Community Server 3.0.

Everything that you require to execute Community Server on a development machine is discussed in *Chapter 2*. The steps required for download and installation of Community Server are explained in depth. The chapter also lists the steps required to configure your installation and describes the various options found in the Control Panel.

One of the greatest features available with Community Server, blogs, is explored in *Chapter 3*. It examines how to create and manage blogs to publish content with the help of a sample blog. It also explains how to configure blogs for registered users.

Community Server has a fully featured discussion forum. *Chapter 4* teaches you how to create forum groups so that you can file each forum under the appropriate group and create a sample forum. After creating forums the chapter covers making posts and also how to manage and administer these forums.

*Chapter 5* shows you how to add a gallery to your Community Server. You will learn how to create photo and file galleries and manage them with the help of sample photo and file galleries.

*Chapter 6* explains the powerful reader and roller features of Community Server. By implementing reader and roller functionality in your site, you can keep track of content of the other blogs using RSS feeds.

*Chapter 7* looks at management of site members, their profiles, resetting passwords, and managing roles, cookies, and avatar settings.

The standard look and feel of Community Server gets a face-lift in *Chapter 8*. It gives you a run down of how attractive Community Server can be through the use of themes and also explains how to make important modifications to your chosen theme. It also teaches you how to use add-ons and modules, and to include custom links in the navigation bar of the site.

*Chapter 9* gives you the edge when it comes to managing various Community Server settings. It explains the management of different settings associated with RSS, post, date, time, and email. At the end of the chapter you learn how to track the IP addresses of visitors to your Community Server site.

*Chapter 10* takes you one step further by looking at the reporting functionality. This chapter shows you how an administrator can generate and view not only user, blog, and forum activity reports but also different types of exceptions and jobs reports.

*Chapter 11* delves into monetizing your site by advertising through Google AdSense and Amazon affiliate programs. It further discusses the management of licenses, word filters, spam blocker, member points, emoticons, and IP addresses.

*Appendix A* walks through the steps followed for deploying Community Server to a hosted server. Basically it provides a sound process for taking the finished product and making it available for public consumption on your host site.

# What You Need for This Book

The prerequisite for this book is a working installation of Community Server. To run Community Server the typical environment consists of IIS (5.1 or greater), .NET Framework (1.1 or greater), a Database System (SQL Server 2000, SQL Server 2005, or SQL Server 2005 Express Edition) and a Development Environment (Visual Studio .NET 2003, Visual Studio 2005, or Visual Web Developer 2005 Express Edition). We cover the details of prerequisites and installation of Community Server in Chapter 2.

# Conventions

In this book, you will find a number of styles of text that distinguish between different kinds of information. Here are some examples of these styles, and an explanation of their meaning.

There are two styles for code. Code words in text are shown as follows: "You can also modify the background color of the page header and other adjoining areas by supplying the appropriate value for the `background-color` property."

A block of code will be set as follows:

```
body, html
{
    margin: 0px;
    padding: 0px;
    color: #000000;
    font-family: Tahoma, Arial, Helvetica;
    background-color: #999966;
}
```

When we wish to draw your attention to a particular part of a code block, the relevant lines or items will be made bold:

```
body, html
{
    margin: 0px;
    padding: 0px;
    color: #000000;
```

```
font-family: Tahoma, Arial, Helvetica;
background-color: #999966;
}
```

**New terms** and **important words** are introduced in a bold-type font. Words that you see on the screen, in menus or dialog boxes for example, appear in our text like this: "clicking the **Next** button moves you to the next screen".

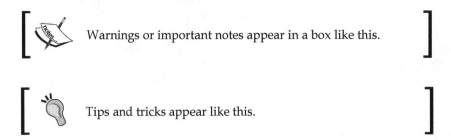

Warnings or important notes appear in a box like this.

Tips and tricks appear like this.

# Reader Feedback

Feedback from our readers is always welcome. Let us know what you think about this book, what you liked or may have disliked. Reader feedback is important for us to develop titles that you really get the most out of.

To send us general feedback, simply drop an email to feedback@packtpub.com, making sure to mention the book title in the subject of your message. You can even submit a review on Amazon.com.

If there is a book that you need and would like to see us publish, please send us a note in the **SUGGEST A TITLE** form on www.packtpub.com or email suggest@packtpub.com.

If there is a topic that you have expertise in and you are interested in either writing or contributing to a book, see our author guide on www.packtpub.com/authors.

# Customer Support

Now that you are the proud owner of a Packt book, we have a number of things to help you to get the most from your purchase.

# Companion Website

Visit the companion website created by the author http://www.communityserverbook.com/ to catch the latest news on the book.

# Errata

Although we have taken every care to ensure the accuracy of our contents, mistakes do happen. If you find a mistake in one of our books—maybe a mistake in text or code—we would be grateful if you would report this to us. By doing this you can save other readers from frustration, and help to improve subsequent versions of this book. If you find any errata, report them by visiting http://www.packtpub.com/support, selecting your book, clicking on the **Submit Errata** link, and entering the details of your errata. Once your errata have been verified, your submission will be accepted and the errata added to the list of existing errata. The existing errata can be viewed by selecting your title from http://www.packtpub.com/support.

# Questions

You can contact us at questions@packtpub.com if you are having a problem with some aspect of the book, and we will do our best to address it.

# 1
# Introducing Community Server

In this chapter, we will provide a brief overview of Community Server and also examine the applications included with it. We will further explore the evolution of Community Server including a comparison with **DotNetNuke (DNN)**. Towards the end of the chapter, we will discuss the various editions and licensing options available for Community Server and also provide a sneak preview of some of the key features of upcoming Community Server 3.0.

## What is Community Server?

**Community Server (CS)** is a web-based application completely built with Microsoft's .NET Framework. It is rendered on the browser as an `aspx` file. Community Server is currently serving millions of websites across the World Wide Web.

 `aspx` is the standard extension for web pages developed using ASP.NET.

 The official website of Community Server is
http://www.communityserver.org

Community Server provides a facility to create and manage applications such as blogs, forums, photo galleries, file galleries, reader, and roller from within a single interface. They can be customized as per your requirements.

Community Server uses a single registration system so you only need to register once to work with all applications provided by it.

You can choose which application is to be displayed on the home page by clicking on the **Applications** link under the **Settings** section by selecting the **Administration** link on the **Dashboard**. For instance, you can enable blogs and forums and disable other applications, so that your end users will be able to access only blogs and forums from the site. In the same way, you can enable or disable other applications depending upon your requirements. Let us examine each one of the applications included within Community Server in detail.

# Blog

A blog or a weblog is an online diary. It can be maintained either daily, weekly, or monthly, as per the convenience of the user who manages it. The first blog was started in 1994 and the term weblog was coined by Jorn Barger on December 17, 1997. A blog could focus on a particular subject such as technology, politics, local and international news, or could just contain random musings. Each post on a blog is classified as separate entry, and old blog posts are automatically archived and are available for reading at any time as long as the blog is active on the World Wide Web. A blog post comprises text, images, links to other blogs or web pages, and other media relevant to your blog. Moreover, people use blogs to post articles and related news, such as about their vacation trips, awards, and much more.

Community Server includes an application for the creation and administration of blogs as shown in the following screenshot:

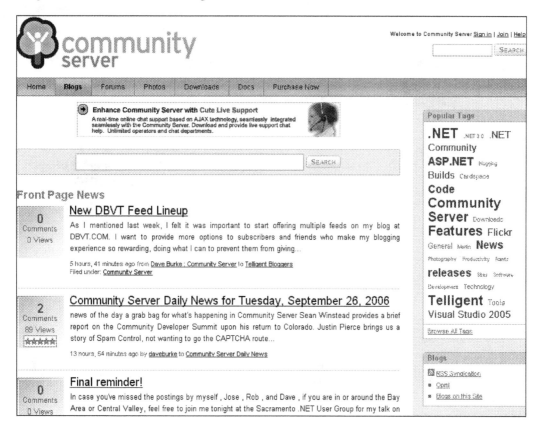

We will examine more about the creation and management of blogs in Chapter 3.

# Forums

A forum is a web-based application used for holding discussions regarding a wide range of topics relevant to the site. The evolution of forums dates back to 1995 when dial-up bulletin boards were popular. Basically, technology, computer games, and health are popular areas for forum themes, but there are forums for a huge number of different topics such as for discussing the features of specific software, programming languages, upcoming events, user-groups discussions, and much more. You should note that a forum relates to a specific topic. Forums are also commonly referred to as message boards, discussion boards, discussion forums, discussion groups, or bulletin boards. Community Server includes an application for the creation, management, and administration of forums as shown in screenshot below:

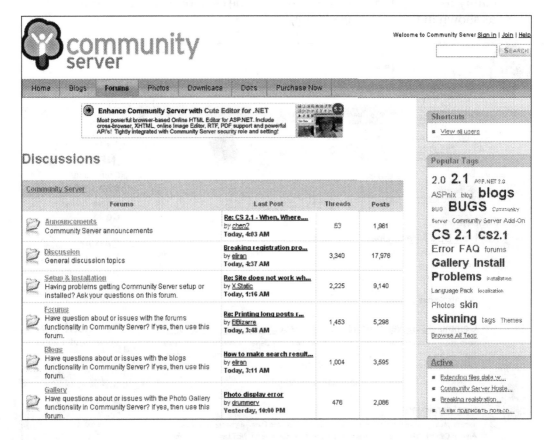

We will examine more about the creation and management of forums in Chapter 4.

# Photo Gallery

A gallery is a term used for storing some kind of information. A photo gallery, as the name suggests, stores photos. In olden days, they were stored as hard copy volumes spanned into several albums. With the evolution of technology, people started storing them on the World Wide Web. Community Server includes an application for the creation, management, and administration of a photo gallery as shown in the screenshot below:

# File Gallery

A file gallery is similar to the photo gallery that we discussed above, with the difference that files are stored inside the file gallery instead of images as in the photo gallery. With Community Server, you can create a file gallery (see the screenshot overleaf) within minutes by following a few simple instructions.

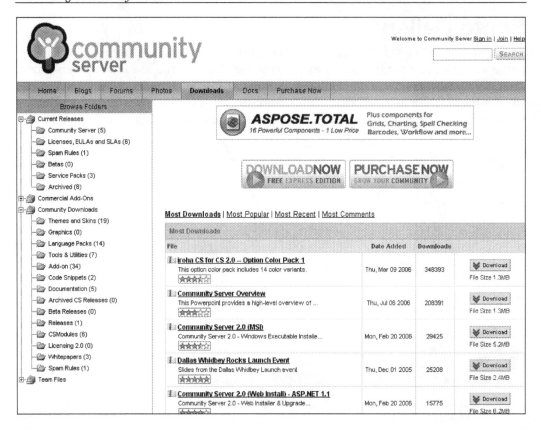

We will examine more about the creation and management of galleries in Chapter 5.

# Reader and Roller

The functionality of reader and roller has been completely overhauled in Community Server 2.1. You will notice significant changes in its working if you currently use any of the previous versions of Community Server.

Reader enables you to display the posts from different blogs using **Really Simple Syndication (RSS) feeds**. It shows the posts together with the relevant links in a grid as shown in the following screenshot. Each registered member of the site can manage his or her own reader provided that the necessary permissions are given by the site administrator.

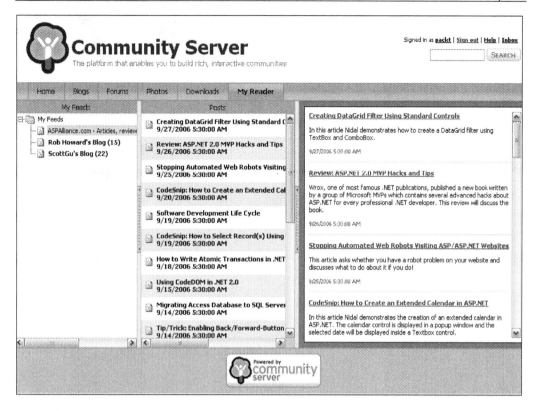

Many people blog everyday with lots of interesting content on a wide range of topics. You can easily display all those external posts in your blog using Community Server and this functionality is termed **roller**. Roller makes use of RSS feeds but the contents are populated inside the relevant blog to which the feed has been added. This feature is popularly called **Content Mirroring**.

We will examine more about the creation and management of reader and roller in Chapter 6.

# The Evolution

Microsoft released the first version of an ASP.NET-based forum application (see screenshot below) in 2002. The application was initially developed by Scott Mitchell under the name WebForums.NET in 2001 and later sold to Microsoft with some additional features. It was first deployed at the official website of ASP.NET and can be downloaded from `http://asp.net/Forums/Download/Default.aspx?tabindex=0&tabid=1`.

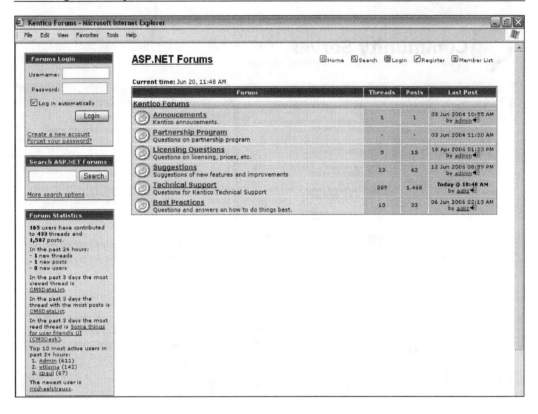

Rob Howard and his team of developers were instrumental in the development and management of the application at Microsoft. The forum software is still being used by many websites and is available separately for download from the above- mentioned Uniform Resource Locator (URL) along with its complete source code.

Rob floated his own company named Telligent Systems in 2004. Telligent decided to develop a new forum application with rich features from scratch. This marked the beginning of Community Server. The development team decided to extend the traditional forum application to include blogs, photos, and galleries, which are relevant for developers, business owners, and hobbyists so that they will get all the required functionalities under a single umbrella. This will also avoid the pain of installing multiple applications for the creation and management of blogs, forums, and galleries.

Telligent initially launched a series of builds and finally ended up with 1.0. After getting the feedback from visitors, Telligent launched Community Server 1.1 including more features. With the release of each version, new features such as an improved user interface and the facility to easily customize the software were included. The launch of Community Server 2.0 has been greatly welcomed among developer circles, since it shipped with many more intuitive features than its earlier counterparts. One such notable feature is that of roller. With roller, you can display posts from the blogs maintained by other people.

> You can either install a fresh copy of Community Server or can upgrade from any of the earlier versions by following the instructions that are included with the installation package.

Telligent has made exciting improvements to version 2.1 of Community Server and it includes many powerful features including a new functionality called Tagging as shown in the screenshot below:

Moreover, all users can create and manage their own reader and the roller, as functionality has been tightly integrated with blogs.

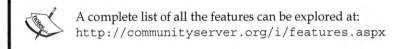

A complete list of all the features can be explored at:
`http://communityserver.org/i/features.aspx`

Telligent has made exciting promises for the future builds of the product, which include an integrated **Content Management System** (**CMS**). We will explore the features included with the upcoming Community Server 3.0 at the end of this chapter.

# A Comparison with DotNetNuke (DNN)

DotNetNuke, popularly called DNN is a robust ASP.NET based application used to build a complete website.

The official website of DotNetNuke can be accessed at `http://www.dotnetnuke.com`.

You will find sites powered with DotNetNuke all over the Web. One of the unique features of DotNetNuke is that users can build and customize their site very easily using administration tools provided by the application. Moreover, advanced developers can tweak the source codes and implement their own functionalities. One such classic example of advanced customization is DotNetPanel (`http://www.dotnetpanel.com`). It is a powerful hosting control panel for managing Windows 2003 Servers.

DotNetNuke ships with a simple discussion board but it does not contain all the features of Community server. It is not possible to create a blog or photo and file galleries using DotNetNuke. On the other hand, Community Server is mainly used for the creation of blogs, forums, photo and file galleries, reader, and for showcasing external blogs using roller. You can make use of both DotNetNuke and Community Server to create high quality website by taking advantage of the rich features provided by both applications. You can easily deploy them on a single website under two different directories since the technology used by both DotNetNuke and Community Server is ASP.NET. You only require a server that supports ASP.NET and SQL Server 2000 or greater. While DotNetNuke is available free of cost without any restrictions, Community Server is available as both free and paid for versions. The free version of Community Server is called *Express* and it has certain restrictions for usage. You will learn more about the different editions in the next section of this chapter.

A complete discussion regarding DotNetNuke is beyond the scope of this book. You are advised to refer to the books *Building Websites with VB.NET and DotNetNuke 3.0* by Daniel N. Egan (ISBN 1-904811-27-2) and *Building Websites with VB.NET and*

*DotNetNuke 4* by Daniel N. Egan, Michael A. Washington, and Steve Valenzula (ISBN 1-904811-99-X) published by Packt Publishing.

# Editions and Licensing

Community Server is available in five different editions: Express, Standard, Professional, Enterprise, and Hosted. Each edition is licensed on a per server basis and includes more features than its predecessors.

 The latest version of the licensing guide is available for download from the **Files** section at `http://communityserver.org/`.

It is possible to upgrade to the higher editions as and when necessary by going through the Upgrade guide available for download from the official website. A brief overview of each edition is given below.

## Express

The Express edition is perfect for people who need to get a community up and running on a budget. It is free, but has restrictions on use. However, it can be deployed for commercial purposes.

## Standard

The Standard edition is the entry-level commercial platform and unlocks some features not available in the Express edition.

## Professional

The Professional edition is targeted at organizations that require many of the capabilities offered by Community Server for running a high-traffic community.

## Enterprise

The Enterprise edition unleashes the full potential of Community Server and has been designed for organizations that require all of the capabilities found in Community Server.

# Hosted

The Hosted edition enables you to create a professional web community within a few minutes without any need to download Community Server separately. It doesn't require any setup or configuration. The hosted edition is available in three different plans—Standard, Plus, and Platinum. You need to purchase any one of these plans by visiting `https://www.communityserver.com/`. You will be provided with a special URL in the format – `http://Domain.communityserver.com`, where `Domain` stands for the name that you gave at the time of registration.

The required disk space and the monthly bandwidth will be provided by Telligent from its servers. This edition is mainly suitable for non-technical people or organizations that want to get a basic Community Server site up and running as quickly as possible without any major effort. Over the coming months Telligent is planning to roll out a number of new capabilities such as integrated email, new themes, as well as a potential free ad-enabled version.

The table given below lists the features included with each edition and also the cost for obtaining each server license:

|  | Express | Standard | Professional | Enterprise |
|---|---|---|---|---|
| Web Sites per server | Unlimited | 1 | 10 | Unlimited |
| Users per license | Unlimited | Unlimited | Unlimited | Unlimited |
| Forums per license | Unlimited | Unlimited | Unlimited | Unlimited |
| Blogs per license | Unlimited | Unlimited | Unlimited | Unlimited |
| Photos per license | Unlimited | Unlimited | Unlimited | Unlimited |
| Files per site | 50 | 500 | Unlimited | Unlimited |
| RSS Reader (Users) | 250 | Unlimited | Unlimited | Unlimited |
| Footer Customization | Not Permitted | Permitted | Permitted | Permitted |
| Spam Blocker | Included | Included | Included | Included |
| IP-Banning Add-on | No | Yes | Yes | Yes |
| Member Points System | No | Yes | Yes | Yes |
| Reports | No | Yes | Yes | Yes |
| Web Farm Support | No | Yes | Yes | Yes |
| Single sign-on Authentication Add-ons | No | No | 1 Available | All Available |
| Email Gateway | No | No | 25 License | 100 License |

| | Express | Standard | Professional | Enterprise |
|---|---|---|---|---|
| Enterprise Search | No | Separate Add-on Available | Included | Included |
| NNTP News Gateway | No | Separate Add-on Available | Separate Add-on Available | 100 License |
| FTP Gateway | No | Separate Add-on Available | Separate Add-on Available | 100 License |
| Microsoft Exchange Connector | No | Separate Add-on Available | Separate Add-on Available | Included |
| Premier Support (Tier 1) | No | No | No | 10 Hours |
| Peer-to-Peer Support (Through Forums) | Yes | Yes | Yes | Yes |
| Cost (US Dollars) | Free | $299 | $1,499 | $9,999 |

 You can purchase a license for the latest version of Community Server at: https://store.telligentsystems.com/

# What's New in Community Server 3.0 (or Calypso)?

Telligent has already announced plans for the release of Community Server 3.0. The version has been code named as **Calypso**. It will be mainly targeted towards simplifying common tasks with intuitive wizards, improvement of user interfaces, and adding more help-oriented content. Moreover, Community Server 3.0 will only run on ASP.NET 2.0, unlike Community Server 2.0 which ran on both ASP.NET 1.1 and 2.0.

The key features that are proposed to be included with Community Server 3.0 are listed overleaf.

# Chameleon

This is a theme engine that will deliver a simpler way to create themes. It will also include features that will enable users to manage the look/feel of a theme via the **Control Panel**. The goals are to reduce the number of files involved in skinning a blog and to provide a streamlined non-technical set of tools for easily creating user interfaces.

# Morpheus

This is a membership update tool, which will be integrated with the ASP.NET 2.0 membership store. This will allow easier integration with existing user bases and external storage of membership data.

# Zion

This is a new centralized file storage system, which will provide more consistent and extensible support for files and attachments in Community Server. In addition, the update to blogs will allow for better image/file support on a per-post basis.

# Tallyman

It is the next version of the mail gateway, which will enable anyone, anywhere, including shared hosting and smaller sites, to leverage integrated email and mail list functionality within Community Server.

Telligent is planning to add one more module to Community Server 3.0, which is code-named **Mystique**. In addition to the above set of new features, Community Server 3.0 also includes an integrated CMS, which will provide knowledge management, content management, and case management functionalities. At the time of writing this book, Calypso is slated for release during the first quarter of 2007.

# Summary

In this chapter, we have seen a brief overview of Community Server and the applications in it. We also explored the evolution of Community Server, a brief comparison with DotNetNuke, and the various editions of the product and features included with each one of them including pricing information. We also examined the new features included with the upcoming Community Server 3.0.

The next chapter will provide a comprehensive coverage of the various steps involved with the installation of Community Server.

# 2
# Getting Started with Community Server

Before beginning to work with Community Server, we need to complete certain initial steps such as installation and configuration of the databases. This chapter demonstrates all the required steps involved with setting up Community Server using Windows and Web-based installation file formats. Towards the end of this chapter, we will demonstrate how to test the installation, and also explore the options included inside the Control Panel Dashboard of Community Server.

## Prerequisites

In order to install and run Community Server, you require access to a set of software as listed below:

| System/Software | Requirements |
| --- | --- |
| Production | Windows Server 2003 or Windows Server 2000 |
| Development | Windows XP Professional with Service Pack 2 |
| Internet Information Services (IIS) | IIS 5.1 or greater |
| .NET Framework | 1.1 or greater |
| Database | SQL Server 2000, SQL Server 2005, or SQL Server 2005 Express Edition |
| Development Environment | Visual Studio .NET 2003, Visual Studio 2005, or Visual Web Developer 2005 Express Edition |

Any one of the development environments listed above will be required for customization of the source code using **Community Server Software Development Kit (SDK)**.

 This chapter assumes that you have installed .NET Framework 1.1 and Community Server 2.1. However, Community Server 3.0, which is the next release, only supports .NET Framework 2.0 or greater.

# Downloading Community Server

The first step that you need to follow is to properly obtain the required software from the official website, http://www.communityserver.org. From the home page, locate the **Downloads** link to find a list of all the latest installations and other companion files, including Community Server Software Development Kit (SDK) as noted earlier. As stated in the previous chapter, you can download the Express Edition, which is available free of cost.

Before initiating a download, you must register on the site. For this purpose, navigate to the above-mentioned site, and click on the link titled **Join,** located on the extreme top of the right-hand side of the page as shown below:

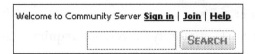

You need to enter the requested details such as **Sign in Name**, **Password**, and **Email Address**. For the purpose of our discussion, we will give the sign-in name as *csbook*. You should enter the password and email address twice and also pick up your preferred **Timezone**. After entering all the required information, click the **Join Now** button to proceed further with the registration process. The button will be enabled only if you enter all the required information on the page. If the registration is successful, you will view a page as shown in the following screenshot and you will be signed in automatically.

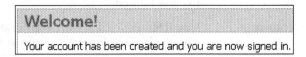

You can browse the Downloads page without registration, but you will be able to download the files only if you register and sign in to the site.

The top right side portion of the page will now read as **Signed in as << User_Name >>** as shown in the following screenshot:

# Install Options

Before downloading the required file for installation, you should locate it properly. For this purpose, click the **Downloads** link from the top navigation bar. Initially, you will be presented with a page that displays a list of all the popular downloads. In order to view the installation files for Community Server 2.1, you need to expand the tree labeled **Current Releases** and select the option titled **Community Server**.

Community Server is available in two different install options—Windows Installer (MSI Format) and Web Installer (ZIP Format). Let us examine the download process involved with each of these file formats in detail.

# Using Windows Installer to Download Community Server

On clicking the link titled **Community Server 2.1 (MSI) - ASP.NET 1.1** from the Downloads page as described earlier, a screen as shown in the screenshot below is displayed:

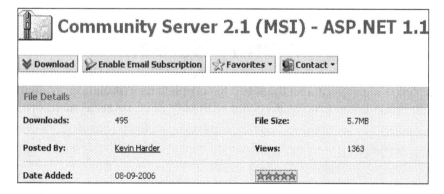

> If you wish to download the installation file for ASP.NET
> 2.0, then you should click the link titled **Community Server
> 2.1 (MSI) - ASP.NET 2.0**.

The download process will be started as soon as you click the **Download** button, and
will be completed within few minutes depending upon the speed of your Internet
connectivity. You should then execute the file in order to install Community Server.
It is not possible to use the installer if you want to upgrade the existing version
of Community Server to a new version or to set it up in a shared web hosting
environment. It is only oriented for fresh installation of Community Server either in
a local system or in an intranet environment.

## Using Web Installer to Download Community Server

The web-based installation package is ideal for setting up Community Server either
in a local system or in a remote web server. In order to download the installation
file, navigate to the **Downloads** page as explained earlier and click the link titled
**Community Server 2.1 (Web Install) - ASP.NET 1.1**. A similar screen to that shown
on the previous page will be displayed.

> If you wish to download the installation file for ASP.NET
> 2.0, then you should click the link titled **Community Server
> 2.0 (Web Install) - ASP.NET 2.0**.

We will examine the process involved with the installation of Community Server
using the two different formats discussed above in the forthcoming sections of
this chapter.

## Installing Community Server

We have now downloaded the required files for installation of Community Server.
The next step is to properly run the setup to complete its installation. We will
examine the installation process involved with both file formats as mentioned above,
in detail.

# Installing Community Server Using the Windows Installer

Since the Windows Installer file format comes in a zipped format, you need to extract the content of it to a location, preferably in a new folder on your hard drive. Once the file has been unzipped, a new file with the name `communityserver_2_1_aspnet11` will be added to the folder in which you extracted the ZIP file. The installation file is a Microsoft Windows Installer Package and hence you can directly start the installation process by double-clicking on it.

In order to extract the contents of a ZIP file, you can either use the built-in compression utility available with the Windows Operating System or one of the third-party software such as WinZip (`http://www.winzip.com`) or JustZIPit (`http://www.download.com/JustZipIt/3000-2250-10222610.html`).

You will then be presented with a series of wizards. You have to follow the instructions specified on the screen to properly install the application. You will be required to accept a license agreement and should also specify a location on your hard drive where the application will be installed. You can also choose the default location. Finally, the installation will be started and the wizard will display the installation progress.

# Configuring Community Server

Once the installation has been successfully completed, the wizard will automatically prompt you to configure Community Server. You need to again go through a series of steps to complete the configuration. The wizard will prompt you to specify the location of the virtual directory, database credentials, and administrator's login information. You can give any meaningful name in **Install** to the virtual folder field on the Web Server Setup screen but the name should not clash with any of the previous installations. After gathering the requested information, the wizard will automatically execute database scripts, which include Tables and Stored Procedures and will prepare the application ready for launch.

A Virtual Directory is a folder on your hard drive mapped to the Internet Information Services (IIS) on your system.

# Connecting to the Database

During the configuration process, you will be asked to specify the required credentials to connect to the SQL Server database as shown in the following screenshot. Firstly, you need to specify the server name or IP address. By default, the server name is (**local**). You should substitute the **Server Name** field with the correct value if you are using Microsoft SQL Server 2005.

 You can retrieve the server name of your SQL Server 2005 installation from the SQL Server Management Studio (**Start | All Programs | Microsoft SQL Server 2005 | SQL Server Management Studio**) login screen.

Instead of creating a new database using SQL Server, you can directly specify the database name along with the required **Username** and **Password**. The wizard will automatically create the specified database and Community Server will be installed under that database.

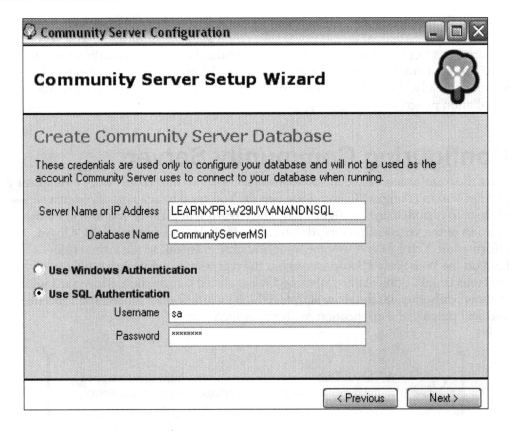

From the screenshot opposite, you should note that the **Username** for setting up the SQL Server database is sa, which stands for System Administrator. The sa, or equivalent account, should only be used for setting up the database, not as the login with which Community Server communicates with the database. In the next screen, you will be required to choose either **Windows Authentication** or **SQL Authentication**. For the purpose of our discussion, you should select the option titled **Use SQL Authentication** and supply the same username and password as you gave in the above step.

# Windows Authentication vs. SQL Server Authentication

Windows integrated authentication is the preferred method for running Community Server. You should configure a single Windows user account for your Community Server system that Community Server can use to communicate with the database. Ideally, this is the same account that IIS uses to run the Community Server application; by default this will be either: ASPNET (Windows 2000 Server) or the Network Service group (Windows Server 2003). SQL Server authentication is used when Windows authentication is not available.

# Configuring the Administrator Account

Once the required database has been successfully created, Community Server will automatically prompt you to specify certain information such as username, password, and email address as shown in the following screenshot overleaf. You will later on use these credentials to log in to the site as an administrator.

 Make sure to specify a password that satisfies the condition listed above in red color. The wizard will not proceed further until you specify a password in the correct format.

After the completion of the configuration, the wizard automatically prompts you to launch the site as shown in the following screenshot.

You can view the installation log by selecting the link **View Installation Log**. The log file specifies the start and end time of various actions performed by the Windows Installer during the installation process.

# Launching Community Server

Community Server will automatically launch in your default browser as seen in the following screenshot, if you had checked the **Launch Community Server** option during the installation process.

The whole installation process has been completely managed by a series of wizards, and there is no need for any manual intervention, even for creation of the database. As noted earlier in the chapter, the above installation process is oriented only for setting up Community Server either locally or in an intranet environment.

On a remote web server, you have to manually install Community Server using the web-based installer, which is available in ZIP format. You can also use the installer for local installation but you should follow certain steps as explained in the next section.

# Installing Community Server Using the Web Installer

Firstly, you have to download the installation file and extract the contents to the root directory (Inetpub/wwwroot), as explained previously. In case you plan to install Community Server on a remote web server then you will be required to upload the folders and files inside the Web folder to the wwwroot directory of the appropriate domain. In some servers, you will be required to upload the files inside httpdocs folder.

Refer to Appendix A for more information regarding
how to properly deploy Community Server in different
environments.

As we discussed earlier, there are separate builds available for ASP.NET 1.1 and 2.0
for version 2.1 of Community Server. We will make use of the installation package
meant for ASP.NET 1.1 to demonstrate the installation process in this section. Locate
the downloaded file on your hard drive after downloading it and extract the contents
of the folder.

The extracted folder contains two folders named SqlScripts and Web, some license
agreement files (EULA), and a readme file. The *SQLScripts* folder contains a number
of SQL script files that are mainly used for upgrading from a previous version of
Community Server to the current version, and not for a fresh installation.

The folder named Web contains lots of files and folders, which are required for
successfully running Community Server. You need to copy the contents of this
folder either inside the root directory of your local system (Inetpub/wwwroot), or
upload inside the root directory (wwwroot or httpdocs) on a remote web server. For
the purpose of our discussion, we will examine the installation process as if you are
performing it in a local system.

# Creating a Database Using SQL Server

The next step in the installation process is to create a SQL Server database using SQL
Server. You can use either SQL Server 2000 or SQL Server 2005 to create a database.
For the purpose of our discussion, we will create a database using SQL Server 2005.
It includes a robust interface for the creation and management of databases named
*SQL Server Management Studio*. You can launch it from **Start | All Programs |
Microsoft SQL Server 2005** and log in by supplying the correct **Server name**, **Login**,
and **Password**.

 You should use the credentials of the default administrator
account, which you gave at the time of SQL Server 2005
installation, for the purpose of database creation.

Once you log in to the management studio, pull down the **Databases** tree from the
left side and right-click on it. Select the menu item named **New Database** as shown
in the following screenshot:

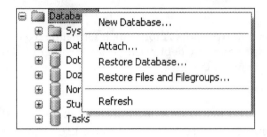

 To create a database using SQL Server 2000, log in to the Query Analyzer as an administrator and supply the following command:

```
create database Your_Database_Name
```

Alternatively, you can also use Enterprise Manager to create the required database.

The **New Database** dialog box pops up. Enter the required database name and click the **OK** button. We will use CommunityServer as a name for our database. SQL Server 2005 will show the progress while the database is being created and will display the same under the **Databases** tree. You can now disconnect from the management studio by selecting **File | Disconnect Object Explorer** menu option.

 SQL Server 2005 Express Edition is available as an alternative to the full blown developer edition of SQL Server 2005. Even though it is free of cost, the main disadvantage of express edition is that the size of each database is restricted to 4 GB. In order to use it, you should download and install Microsoft SQL Server 2005 Express Edition (53.8 MB) and SQL Server Management Studio Express (38.5 MB) from http://msdn.microsoft. com/vstudio/express/sql/download/. Once you have installed both of them, you can log in to SQL Server Management Studio Express by supplying the credentials that you gave at the time of installation of Microsoft SQL Server 2005 Express Edition. The look and feel of the studio interface looks similar to that of developer edition and the process of database creation is also the same as explained above.

We have now successfully created a database required for the installation of Community Server. The next step is to launch the web-based installation wizard to install the application.

Community Server ships with a built-in web-based installer along with the web installer package in ZIP format. It will automatically create the required tables and stored procedures for the successful installation of the application.

# Using the Installation Wizard

By default, the Installation Wizard is disabled and you should enable it before attempting to install Community Server. To enable the installer, you need to navigate to the folder **Installer** inside the **Web** directory and open the **default.aspx** file. You can open the file using any editor of your choice such as Notepad, Visual Studio 2005, or Visual Web Developer 2005 Express Edition.

In the `default.aspx` file, locate the statement

```
bool INSTALLER_ENABLED = false;
```

You should modify the value of the above statement to *true* to enable the installer. You are now ready to launch the web-based installer to install Community Server.

For the purpose of our discussion, we have modified the name of the folder `Web` to `cs21`. Hence, we need to enter `http://localhost/cs21/Installer/default.aspx` on the browser to launch the installation wizard. Now, you will have to fix an error message (see the following screenshot) before proceeding further with the installation process.

This error can be easily resolved by navigating to the folder cs21 using Internet Information Services (IIS) and making it as an application.

Launch Internet Information Services (IIS) by navigating to **Start | Control Panel | Administrative Tools**. Double-click the icon labeled **Internet Information Services** and pull down the server name from the left side panel. Expand the tree labeled **Web Sites | Default Web Site** and locate the folder cs21. Right-click on it and select **Properties**. The following dialog box is displayed:

Click the **Create** button to transform the folder cs21 to an application. The **Application name** field will now display our folder name.

> You will not have to perform this task if you host
> Community Server on a remote web server since the
> root virtual directory will be automatically enabled as an
> application at the time of creation of the site.

We are now ready to launch the installer by navigating to
`http://localhost/cs21/installer/default.aspx`. You will be required to
walk through a series of wizards to proceed with the Community Server installation.
You need to click the **Next** button on each screen to proceed further with the
installation process.

> If you have installed .NET Framework 1.1 and 2.0 and
> version 2.0 is your default framework then the system will
> throw a **The resource cannot be found** error message.
> In order to resolve this error, click the button captioned
> **Configuration** from the IIS Properties dialog and double
> click the extension **.aspx**. The **Add/Edit Application
> Extension Mapping** dialog pops up. In the **Executable**
> field, modify the .NET Framework version number from
> 2.0.50727 to 1.1.4322.

During the course of installation, you will be asked to supply the required
credentials for connecting to the SQL Server database as shown in the
following screenshot:

**Community Server Database Login**
Select the database login that Community Server will use to connect to the database.

IP address or Server Name: `(local)`

○ Windows Authentication

◉ SQL Server Authentication

Username: `sa`

Password: `••••••••`

You need to enter either the actual server name of your local SQL Server installation or the IP address that needs to be connected to if you are running the installer on a remote server. The IP address should be that of your remote SQL Server installation, and not that of the web server. Nowadays, the majority of hosts separate web and database servers to increase the performance of websites. You will need to contact your service provider if you are not sure as to what to give as the server name. We have already discussed Windows Authentication and SQL Server Authentication. If you use SQL Server Authentication then you should supply the required username and password.

If the entered credentials are correct then the installation wizard will automatically populate the SQL Server 2005 databases available on the system. For the purpose of our discussion, we earlier created a database named CommunityServer. If you are running the installation on a remote web server, then the wizard will display the list of all databases available on the remote database server. Click on the **Next** button to continue with the installation process after selecting the appropriate database from the list.

The wizard automatically prompts you to choose the installation options as shown in the following screenshot. It is recommended you checkmark all the options for the sake of simplicity.

Choose Installation Options

Select the installation options below to control how your database is created.

☑ **Script ASP.NET MemberRoles**
This option will create the ASP.NET MemberRoles information and remove the objects if they are already present. If you're installing into a shared database with other MemberRole compatible applications please uncheck this option.

☑ **Script Community Server**
Select this option if you are installing for the first time or you wish to recreate the Community Server schema. If you already have a working schema then please uncheck this option to keep your current schema intact.

☑ **Create Community**
Choose this option to have the installer create a new community for you or if you already have an existing community in the database this will allow you to create another community.

After investigating the above options, click **Next** button to proceed further. The wizard will prompt you to enter the requested information for the creation of an administrator account such as **Username**, **Password,** and an **Email** address as shown in the next screenshot. You will need to log in using these credentials after successful installation to manage Community Server. It is highly advisable to checkmark the entry titled **Create Sample Data** so that the wizard will automatically create a sample blog and a photo gallery. You can simply leave the **Community Url** field as it is without any modifications. Community Server automatically populates this field with the required web address as shown in the following screenshot:

The installer will automatically create tables, stored procedures, and the required sample data as soon as you click the **Next** button from the screen in the above screenshot. This process may take some time to complete, and a page with the required link for navigating to the home page will be displayed after the completion of the installation process.

The remote web server sometimes displays a timeout error when you perform the above installation step. In such a case, you should attempt to perform the installation at a time when the server traffic is not at its peak. You must either delete the current database and create a new one when you install again or just create a new one at the time when you again perform the installation process. Otherwise, the installation will not be successful.

You have now successfully completed the installation of Community Server.

If you used the Web Installer for performing the installation process, it is highly recommended that you remove the folder **Installer**. Alternatively, you can disable the installation wizard by undoing the changes we made to the **default.aspx** file earlier. This will enable you to again run the installation wizard if required at a later point of time.

# Testing the Installation of Community Server

Since we have successfully completed the installation process, let us now look at how to test and view the final output. For this purpose, navigate to `http://localhost/cs21` using your browser.

You may receive a **Directory Access Denied** error message when you attempt to access the site using the above-mentioned address. To fix this error first navigate to **Start | Control Panel | Administrative Tools | Internet Information Services**. Then locate the folder `cs21`, right-click, select **Properties**, and then choose the **Documents** tab as shown in the screenshot below:

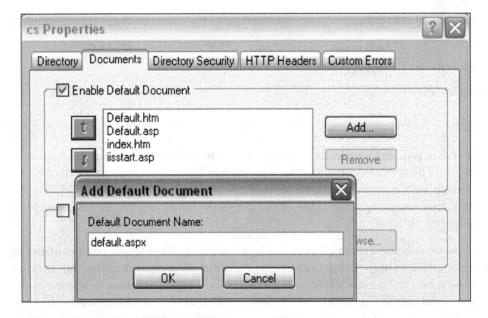

Initially, **default.aspx** is not added as a default document inside the default documents list box. You can add it by selecting the **Add** button and entering the required file name as shown in the screenshot opposite. You will not get the above-mentioned error message when you install Community Server using Windows Installer. This is because the installer automatically configures the relevant Virtual Directory during the installation process.

We have already seen the final output earlier (see the screenshot that is a 'Welcome' page, in the section *Launching Community Server*) when we discussed the installation of Community Server using Windows Installer file package. At the top of the home page, you will see five links as shown below:

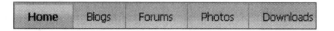

You should note that a sample Blog and a Photo gallery have been automatically created by the installer. You can set up remaining applications such as forums or photo and file galleries using the administration control panel. We will examine the creation and management of all applications included within Community Server in the following chapters.

# Navigating the Control Panel Dashboard

The Control Panel is the main brain behind the working of Community Server. In order to work with the Control Panel, you need to log in as an administrator. This can be done by clicking on the **Sign in** link located on the top of the page and by entering your administrator username and password, which you gave at the time of installation.

As soon as you log in, you will be able to view a new link titled **Control Panel** as shown in the screenshot below:

If you click the **Control Panel** link, you will see lot of settings for managing all the applications included with Community Server. These settings are displayed in a page titled **Dashboard**, which displays all the required functionalities for managing the site. The following table shows a list of all the options included on the **Dashboard** along with its purpose:

| Control Panel Dashboard options | Purpose |
| --- | --- |
| Membership | To manage users registered on the site |
| My Blog(s) | To create and edit post<br>To manage comments |
| Blog Administration | To add new blogs<br>To manage permissions |
| My Photo(s) | To add new photos<br>To manage albums and comments |
| Photo Administration | To create new gallery<br>To manage permissions |
| My File(s) | To upload and manage files<br>To manage sub-folders and comments |
| File Administration | To create new folders<br>To manage permissions |
| Forums Moderation | To moderate forums |
| Forums Administration | To create new forums<br>To manage permissions |
| Reader Administration | To manage external feeds<br>To manage permissions |
| System Administration | To manage the whole site<br>To generate and view reports |

You can also individually explore these options by clicking on the relevant links located on the top navigation bar inside the control panel as shown in the following screenshot:

| Dashboard | My Blogs | My Photos | My Files | Forums Moderation | Administration | Reporting |

On the right side of the Dashboard, you will find announcements, which are updated regularly by Telligent, and also the version number of Community Server. You can return to the home page at any time by clicking on the link labeled **Exit Control Panel and Return to Site** located on the top portion of the control panel dashboard as shown in the screenshot below:

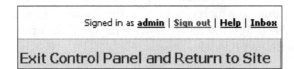

Signed in as **admin** | **Sign out** | **Help** | **Inbox**

Exit Control Panel and Return to Site

# Summary

In this chapter, we looked at the installation of Community Server using both the Windows Installer (MSI) and Web Installer (ZIP) packages. We also saw how to load Community Server after its successful installation and also briefly explored the options found inside the control panel dashboard.

From the next chapter onwards, we will start exploring each one of the applications included with Community Server starting from the creation and management of blogs.

# 3
# Working with Blogs

In the previous chapters, we examined the evolution of Community Server and its installation procedure, and also gave a brief outline of the various elements included within the **Dashboard**. From this chapter onwards, we will begin our adventure with the various applications included with Community Server. In this chapter, we will discuss the creation and management of blogs with the help of a sample blog.

## Understanding Blogs

A blog is a simple tool for people to quickly and easily publish content. Posts to a blog can span any topic from reviews, vacation news, family events and happenings to work-related issues, etc. They can be about any issue that relates to the daily activities of a person, group, or organization. Also, other readers can post their opinions or feedback as comments on these blog entries. In short, a blog is a place to conveniently share ideas and publish thoughts. Community Server archives posts automatically on a monthly basis.

There are a number of websites that provide a facility to easily create and set up a blog such as Blogger (http://www.blogger.com) from Google. From such websites, you can create your own blog instantly. Many companies have also developed blog-related applications where the users can plug in to their own web space. This gives more flexibility to users as they can manage their blog themselves instead of accessing it by using another URL. Community Server ships with a powerful blog application with which users can create and manage blogs for themselves or for their friends, customers, and employees. We will thoroughly examine all the aspects of building a blog using Community Server in this chapter.

We will analyze the concepts surrounding Community Server blogs with the help of a sample blog titled *csbook*. We will then explore how to manage the blog, post content, and format blog posts, along with other related topics.

# Blog Groups

Before we create a blog, we need to create a blog group. Blog groups are a way of organizing blogs within the site. For our understanding, we'll create a new blog group *csbookblog* for our blog.

## Creating a Blog Group

In order to create a blog group, click on the link titled **Blog Groups** located under the **Blogs** navigation panel by selecting the **Administration** link on the Dashboard. You will view a new page as shown in the following screenshot. From the following screenshot, you will see that a sample blog group with the name **Sample Weblogs** has been automatically created by the installer.

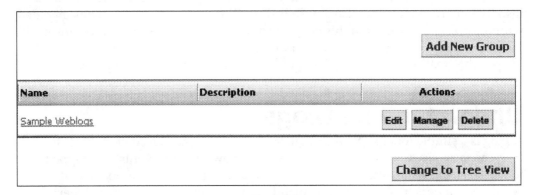

Now, click the **Add New Group** button. A small window with the title **New Group** will pop up. Enter the required information in it as shown in the screenshot below and submit the page by clicking on the **Save** button.

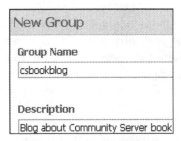

You will be returned to the **Site Administration** page and the newly created blog group will appear below the default group as shown in the next screenshot:

| Name | Description | | Actions | | |
|---|---|---|---|---|---|
| Sample Weblogs | | | Edit | Manage | Delete |
| csbookblog | Blog about Community Server book | | Edit | Manage | Delete |

# Managing Blog Groups

You can edit or delete a blog group at any time. Editing a blog group is very similar to creating a new group but deleting it is a little different. Community Server will prompt you to confirm the action by showing a message box that lets you cancel the operation if you had clicked the button by mistake.

In the same manner, you can create a number of blog groups as per your requirements. For instance, you can create separate groups for each programming language so that you can file each blog under the respective group. This will help you to manage the blog easily at a later point of time. Community Server is designed to support thousands of blogs on a single installation, so while the necessity of a blog group isn't immediately apparent, if you run a larger site, it will be invaluable.

By default, the **Site Administration** page is displayed in grid view. You can change the look to tree view by clicking on the button captioned **Change to Tree View**. The big advantage of using the tree view interface is that you can perform various tasks very much more easily than from the default grid view interface.

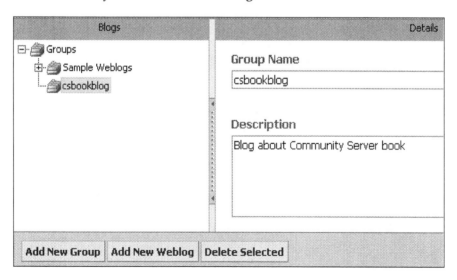

Adding a new group is very easy with the tree view interface. The relevant fields will be displayed on the **Blogs** and **Details** sections as soon as you click on the **Add New Group** button. You can easily edit a group by simply clicking on the relevant tree node. You can also right click on the tree to create and manage a blog group. Let us now look into how to create a new blog.

# Creating a Blog

Now we can create the *csbook* sample blog. For this purpose, we have to log on to our Community Server site as an administrator and use the options inside the **Dashboard** to create the blog.

Once you are logged in as the site administrator click on the link labelled **Control Panel** from the top navigation bar. Inside the **Dashboard**, you will see a series of entries as shown in the screenshot below:

Click on the link titled **Add new blogs, control permissions, etc** to begin. You will now view a lot of settings on the left-side navigation panel as shown in the screenshot below. As an administrator, you will use these settings to create and manage blogs.

You can also access **Blog Settings** by clicking the **Administration** link from the **Dashboard**.

In order to follow the steps explained below, you should change the interface to grid view format by clicking on the **Change to Grid View** button located on the bottom right-hand side of the page. Click on the link titled **Create New Blog** located under the **Blogs** section on the navigation panel to create a new blog. You will view a page as shown below:

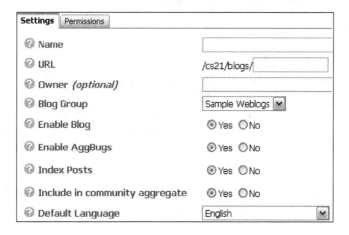

You will have to enter the required information to create a new blog using the various options on the **Settings** tab. You can also specify permissions for the new blog using the **Permissions** tab. If you point the mouse cursor over the question mark symbol, a screen tip will be displayed and this will help you to learn more about that specific setting.

Let us now examine each one of the options included on the **Settings** tab in detail:

**Name**: You need to give a name for your blog. It should be preferably a name that corresponds to the context of your site. For instance, if your site is related to ASP. NET, then you can supply a name such as aspnetblog. For our sample blog, we will give csbook as the name.

**URL**: You should specify a unique value, which will be used to identify your blog. The relevant blog will be created inside the blog's subdirectory located inside your Community Server installation folder. For example, if your Community Server website is http://mygreatsite.com, your URL would be http://mygreatsite.com/blogs/[URL].

For our sample blog, we will give a value `csbook` in the field. Hence, in order to navigate to the blog, we should navigate to `http://localhost/cs21/blogs/csbook` to view the home page of our blog after its creation.

**Owner**: In this field, you can include the username of a member who will manage the blog. The specified member will ultimately become the owner of the blog. For our sample blog, we will specify a member with the username `anandn_mvp` as the owner. Hence, this member can manage our sample blog titled `csbook`.

 Administrators can manage all blogs on the site.

You should note that when you deploy Community Server on a production server, you will have to specify the actual username of a user registered on the site. As an administrator, you should either contact the member for the actual username or can also create a new account for a member directly by clicking the **Create New Account** link located under the **Membership** section inside the **Dashboard**. As soon as the specified user logs in they will have access to the **Dashboard** from where they can post content and manage their blog.

**Blog Group**: You should select the specific blog group from the drop-down list. We have already created a new blog group with the name csbookblog and we will use this group to create our sample blog.

**Enable Blog**: You can enable or disable the blog using this setting. By default, this field is enabled. If you disable it then you will not be able to manage the blog until you enable the blog again. This setting will be useful when you need to do any maintenance on your blog.

**Enable AggBugs**: If you enable this option, then an invisible tracking image will be inserted into each of the syndicated post. This setting is useful for RSS readers that display your post and allows Community Server to maintain statistics on how often RSS readers read your content (although the accuracy of these statistics is usually under reported).

**Index Posts**: This setting will enable the blog posts to be included in search results. The relevant posts will be visible as soon as you perform a search on the Community Server site. However, the blog posts will not be included in the RSS feed.

**Include in community aggregate**: When this option is enabled, all posts are included in the blog home page and also in the RSS feed.

**Default Language**: Community Server provides the ability to select a language for your blog. The default language is English but you can select another language if you prefer.

# Managing Permissions

Community Server supports a robust permission system that allows the site administrator to delegate permissions to other users. The permission system uses role-based authentication; thus users are assigned to roles and roles are then granted permissions to perform tasks.

You can give access to the blog to various users registered on the site using the settings on the tab named **Permissions**. All you need to do is to appropriately select the specific permission for a specific group of users as shown in the following screenshot:

| Name | View | Manange Content | Reply | Ink | Video | Upload Attachment | Remote Attachment |
|------|------|-----------------|-------|-----|-------|-------------------|-------------------|
| BlogAdministrator | ☑ | ☑ | ☑ | ☐ | ☐ | ☑ | ☑ |
| Editor | ☐ | ☐ | ☐ | ☐ | ☐ | ☐ | ☐ |
| Everyone | ☑ | ☐ | ☑ | ☐ | ☐ | ☐ | ☐ |
| FileAdministrator | ☐ | ☐ | ☐ | ☐ | ☐ | ☐ | ☐ |
| ForumsAdministrator | ☐ | ☐ | ☐ | ☐ | ☐ | ☐ | ☐ |
| GalleryAdministrator | ☐ | ☐ | ☐ | ☐ | ☐ | ☐ | ☐ |
| MembershipAdministrator | ☐ | ☐ | ☐ | ☐ | ☐ | ☐ | ☐ |
| Moderator | ☐ | ☐ | ☐ | ☐ | ☐ | ☑ | ☐ |
| Owners | ☑ | ☑ | ☑ | ☐ | ☐ | ☑ | ☑ |
| ReaderAdministrator | ☐ | ☐ | ☐ | ☐ | ☐ | ☐ | ☐ |
| ReaderUser | ☐ | ☐ | ☐ | ☐ | ☐ | ☐ | ☐ |
| Registered Users | ☑ | ☐ | ☑ | ☐ | ☐ | ☐ | ☐ |
| SystemAdministrator | ☑ | ☑ | ☑ | ☐ | ☐ | ☑ | ☑ |
| Trusted Users | ☐ | ☐ | ☐ | ☐ | ☐ | ☐ | ☐ |

For instance, you can give the permission to upload files to a moderator by navigating to the **Moderator** row and clicking on the checkbox in the **Upload Attachment** column.

You need not go back to the **Settings** tab again after specifying permissions. You can directly click on the **Save** button located at the bottom of the page to create a new blog. As soon as you click on the button, the relevant blog will be created and displayed inside the grid as shown in the following screenshot:

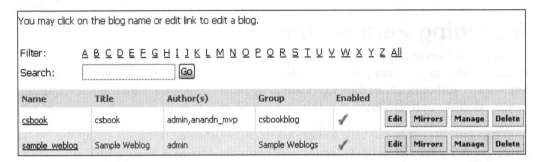

As you can see from the above screenshot, the grid shows the owner(s) (in the column **Author(s)**) of that blog and also the relevant group to which it has been associated. The blog has also been enabled and is ready for use. You can also edit, manage, or delete the blogs at any time by clicking on the relevant button from the specified row on the grid.

 You can globally specify the required permissions for all the active blogs created on the site using the **Global Permissions** link from the **Blogs** section located inside the Site Administration page. To access the Site Administration page, click the **Control Panel** link and then select the **Administration** link.

# Managing a Blog

The blog owner or users identified as blog owners through permissions now have the ability to manage the blog.

 An administrator should specify the permissions for the members registered on the site to access a specific blog during the creation of the blog as discussed in the section *Creating a Blog*.

You can manage a blog created on the site by either clicking on the **Manage** button from the grid on the blogs page or by selecting the **My Blogs** link in the **Control Panel** main navigation user interface. The **Blog Management** page appears with a new navigation panel and other related information as shown in the next screenshot:

| Common Tasks ⌃ | Current Blog: <u>csbook</u> | Select Blog to Manage |
|---|---|---|
| Write a Blog Post | | |
| Create a New Page | | |
| Review Comments | | |
| Manage Content ⌄ | | |
| Global Settings ⌄ | | |

## My Blog Dashboard

┌─ Blog Author(s) and General Statistics ─────────────────────
Author(s):  admin,anandn_mvp
This blog was created on 09-02-2006

┌─ Blog Posts and Pages ───────────────────────────────
Total Posts Published:   0
Total Pages Published:   0

┌─ Feedback ───────────────────────────────────────
Awaiting Approval:                         <u>0</u>
Total Comments:                            <u>0</u>
Total Trackbacks and Pingbacks:  <u>0</u>

The entry **Current Blog** indicates the URL of the active blog. The link title reads **csbook** and it indicates that it is our sample blog. For our sample blog, URL will be `http://localhost/cs21/blogs/csbook/default.aspx`. The **My Blog Dashboard** section provides information about the owner, creation date of the blog, and total number of posts and pages. It also includes feedback-related details such as total number of comments posted on the blog and how many are pending for approval by the administrator including the **Total Trackbacks and Pingbacks**.

Trackback is a method by which two blogs communicate with each other. Community Server provides built-in support for trackbacks. For example, if you publish content on your blog and if there is similar content at another blog then you can notify the owner of that other blog with a trackback ping. The notification will be communicated to the owner of another blog in the form of entries. The trackback value will be updated as other blog owners post content similar to the content that you have posted. The real usage of this feature will be visible only if you run a blog hosted on a live web server.

Pingback is similar to trackback. With the help of pingbacks, you can request notification when somebody links to one of your documents, articles, or posts. This enables you to keep track of who is linking to, or referring to your articles or posts. Community Server supports automatic pingbacks where all the links in a published article can be pinged when the article is published.

The **Select Blog to Manage** button enables you to switch to a blog, if you wish to manage another blog on the site. However, you will only be able to manage only those blogs for which you have permissions.

As you can see from the screenshot on the previous page, the navigation bar on the left side includes various options for managing a blog. Let us now examine each one of them in detail.

# Writing your Blog Entry

In order to author a blog post, you should click the link titled **Write a Blog Post** from the **Common Tasks** panel on the **Blog Management** page. Initially, you will view a text editor as shown in the next screenshot:

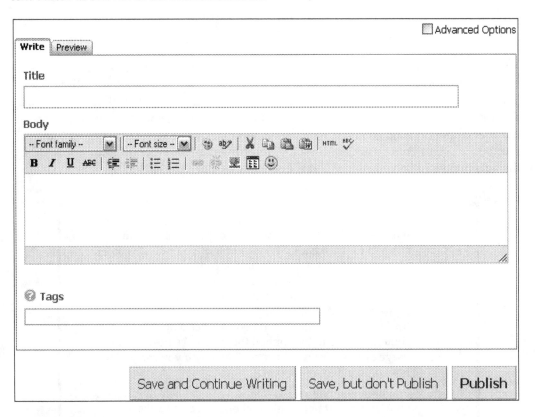

If you select the **Advanced Options** check box from the above displayed interface, you will be able to see a text editor with a new set of tabs as shown in the screenshot below:

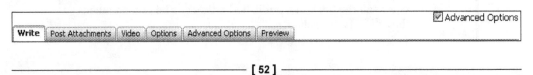

You can post a simple blog by entering the required information in the **Title**, **Body**, and **Tags** fields. If you file a blog entry under a specified tag, then it will enable you to browse the relevant post easily by simply clicking on the specific tag. You can also enhance your content by using the various formatting options available on the text editor.

> By default, you see a standard text editor without any major features. You can modify the interface to an enhanced editor by selecting your username from the top of the page and selecting the required value from the **Content Editor** dropdown located under the **Site Options** tab.

For our sample blog, we will post a simple post with the following information:

| | |
|---|---|
| **Title** | Community Server - A User Guide |
| **Body** | In this book, you will learn how to create and manage Blogs, Forums, Galleries, Downloads using the latest version of Community Server. In addition, you will also learn how to customize and deploy the application. |
| **Tags** | Blogs;Forums;Galleries;Photos;File;CS |

The **Post Attachments** tab enables you to add files to your blog entry. Files added through this tab will also be published as an attachment in the RSS feed for your blog. For example, to create a podcast you could simply attach an audio file here.

You will view two buttons captioned **Add/Update** and **Remove** upon clicking the tab. On clicking the **Add/Update** button, a new dialog with the title **Attach File** pops up as shown in the following screenshot. You can either attach a file from your local system or give a link to a resource on the Web. For our sample blog, we will attach a file located on the local system.

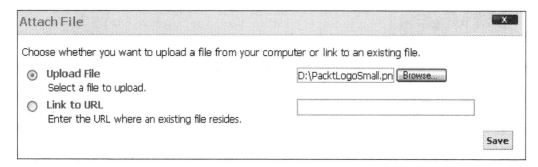

Since we have uploaded an image from the system, we need to select the first option, browse for the file and click on the **Save** button to finish the process.

You can upload videos to your blog, such as a demonstration of your site or a tutorial demo regarding ASP.NET 2.0 or anything that you have created, using the options available on the **Video** tab.

>  You can also click the **Create a New Page** link located under the **Common Tasks** panel on the **Blog Management** page to write a new blog entry.

You can post a short excerpt or an abstract about your blog using the **Options** tab. If you wish to give a unique name for your blog entry then you can make use of the **Name** field. You can also specify the date and time on which the blog has to be posted on the site from the **Options** tab.

The **Advanced Options** tab enables you to manage some of the other activities related to your blog as described in the list given below:

**Allow Replies/Comments**: If this is disabled, your readers can't post comments to your blog entry.

**Comment Moderation**: You can specify whether to moderate comments or not. By default, all comments are published immediately after posting.

**Email Feedback Notifications**: When this is enabled, owners will receive email notifications when new comments are made to their blog. By default, notifications are disabled.

**Enable Trackbacks**: When this is enabled, the blog will record trackbacks and pingbacks.

**Enable Ratings**: Users can rate a post on the scale of 1 to 5, where 5 is the highest rating. By default, rating is enabled for each post.

**Publish to my aggregate list**: If this is enabled, your post will appear on the list of posts on the home page.

**Publish to site's aggregate list**: If this is enabled, your post will be included in the list of posts for you blog.

**Syndicate Excerpt**: If this is enabled, your excerpt will be published in the RSS feed for your blog.

The **Preview** tab will help you to view the post before it is published on the site. For our sample blog the preview will look as shown in the following screenshot:

After previewing the blog entry, you should post it to the system. Community Server provides three different options for posting a blog entry as you can see from the above screenshot.

The **Save and Continue Writing** button not only saves the active blog entry but also enables you to continue composing it without any interruption. This option is beneficial for long blog entries where you could save the post very often to avoid loss of data.

The **Save, but don't Publish** button enables you to save the blog entry. An important point to note is that the blog entry will not be published publicly on the site if you choose this button. The relevant entry will not be visible outside the **Control Panel**. This option is beneficial if you wish to publish the post after updating the blog post at a later time.

The **Publish** button saves and publishes the blog entry publicly on the site. You can choose this option if you have finished the writing process completely.

As soon as you click on the **Publish** button, the relevant blog entry will be visible inside the grid on the Blog Posts page. The grid displays a list of all the published blog posts as shown in the screenshot below. For our sample blog, we have published only one post and hence the grid displays a single post.

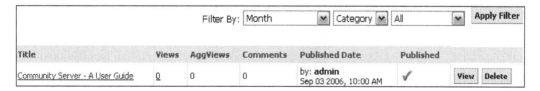

# Viewing a Blog Post

You can view the blog entry by clicking the **View** button from the relevant row on the grid. Alternatively, you can click on the **Current Blog** link on the top of the page to navigate directly to your blog. For our sample blog, the final output as it appears on the home page will look like this:

## Community Server - A User Guide

In this book, you will learn how to create and manage Blogs, Forums, Galleries, Downloads using the latest version of Community Server. In addition, you will also learn how to customize and deploy the application.

Posted <u>Sunday, September 03, 2006 6:00 PM</u> by <u>admin</u> | <u>0 Comments</u> [Edit]
Filed under: <u>Galleries</u>, <u>CS</u>, <u>Photos</u>, <u>Blogs</u>, <u>Forums</u>, <u>File</u> [Edit Tags]

**Attachment(s):** <u>PacktLogoSmall.png</u>

We will explore more about the various items on the home page of the blog in detail later on in this chapter.

# Working with Comments

In the previous section, we saw how to post and view a blog entry. In this section, we will examine how to work with comments that other users post to your blog. But before proceeding further, let us see how to post a comment. Navigate to the home page of the blog as explained in the previous section and click on the link titled **0 Comments[Edit]** on the bottom of the post as displayed in the above screenshot. Enter the required information as shown in the screenshot below and click on the **Submit** button.

The URL field allows you to display your web address on the site and it is optional. You should however compulsorily enter your feedback about the relevant blog post on the **Comments** field if you wish to post a comment

As soon as you click the **Submit** button, Community Server displays a message like: **Thanks for sharing your feedback! If your feedback doesn't appear right away, please be patient as it may take a few minutes to publish - or longer if the blogger is moderating comments.**

The above message signifies that your comment has been successfully posted on the relevant blog. If the blog has been enabled to immediately publish comments, which our sample blog has, you will be able to view the comment if you browse to the relevant blog post. Let us now examine how to view the posted comment.

# Viewing Comments

Comments can be viewed only along with the relevant blog post. There are different ways to view them. If you are inside the **Dashboard** and logged in as an administrator then you need to click the **My Blogs** link from the top navigation bar. From the **My Blog Dashboard** page, navigate to the link titled **Current Blog**. You will be able to view the comment if you click the link that is highlighted in the following screenshot:

If you are outside the **Dashboard** but logged in as an administrator or user then you can directly navigate to the home page of the site and click on the link titled **Blogs** from the top navigation bar. By default, the home page displays a list of all the posts available on the blog as shown in the screenshot overleaf:

As you can see from the screenshot above, one comment has been posted along with the total number of hits (four in our case). The other blog entry has been created by the installer at the time of installation of Community Server.

Clicking on the heading will take you to the relevant blog page. You should note that for each post there is a separate URL, which you can see in the address bar of your browser. For our sample blog post, it will look like `http://localhost/cs21/ blogs/csbook/archive/2006/09/03/Community-Server-_2D00_-A-User-Guide. aspx` and this comment can be viewed by navigating to the URL as follows:

Community Server - A User Guide ☆☆☆☆☆

In this book, you will learn how to create and manage Blogs, Forums, Galleries, Downloads using the latest version of
Community Server. In addition, you will also learn how to customize and deploy the application.

Published Sunday, September 03, 2006 6:00 PM by <u>admin</u> Edit
Filed under: <u>Galleries</u>, <u>CS</u>, <u>Photos</u>, <u>Blogs</u>, <u>Forums</u>, <u>File</u> [Edit Tags]

Attachment(s): <u>PacktLogoSmall.png</u>

**Comment Notification**

<u>Send me email alerts for new comments to this post</u>

<u>Subscribe to this post's comments using RSS</u>

Comments

<u>admin</u> **said:**

Great Work - Anand

September 3, 2006 11:31 AM [Remove this Comment]

As you can see from the above screenshot, the comment is displayed along with the
exact date and time at which it was posted.

# Generating Email Alerts

In order to receive an email alert whenever any new comments are posted to the
blog post, you should click the link titled **Send me email alerts for new comments
to this post** on the **Blog** page. As soon as you click on it, the link title changes to **Stop
sending me email alerts for this post**. You should click on this link to stop receiving
alerts from the site.

# Managing Comments

Let us now examine how to manage comments. Firstly, click on the link **My Blogs**
from the **Dashboard** to open the **Blog Management** page. Select the **Review
Comments** link from the left side navigation bar and the following page will
be displayed:

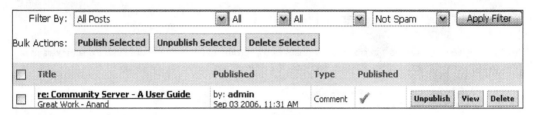

The **View** button will enable you to preview both the post and the comment. You can also delete the comment from the post by using the **Delete** button. By default, the page will show the comments posted on all the blog posts. You can refine them further by using the **Filter By** drop-down list. You can filter comments by the **Post Heading**, its **Type** and also by its **Status**. Some visitors will post unwanted comments. In such cases, the Community Server spamming system automatically isolates those comments and you can search comments based on the spam criteria. The above screenshot implies that the comment that we posted has been published on the site. You can click the **Unpublish** button if you wish not to publish the comment on the site.

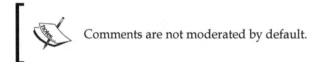

Comments are not moderated by default.

If comment moderation is enabled then the site administrator will have to approve the comment before it is actually published on the blog and the site. In such a case, you can use the **Bulk Actions** button. The **Publish Selected** button instantly posts all the selected comments. The **Unpublish Selected** button instantly removes all the selected comments from the site. You can also use this button to remove a single comment. The **Delete Selected** button immediately deletes all the selected comments from the site.

If you click on the link located under the **Title** column, a window with an enhanced text editor will pop up as shown in the next screenshot. You can directly edit the comment using the provided interface.

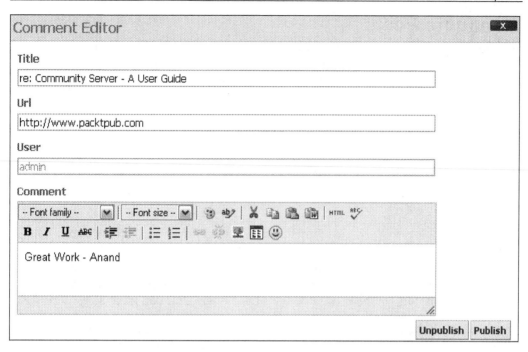

As you can see from the above screenshot, you can decide not to publish the comment using the **Unpublish** button. The updated comment will be published as soon as you click the **Publish** button.

# Managing Content

In order to manage content, you should first navigate to the **Blog Management** page by selecting the **My Blogs** link from the **Dashboard**. Once you are inside the page, select the **Manage Content** link from the navigation panel located on the left-hand side to view the settings on it (see screenshot below).

We have already discussed the **All Comments** option previously in the *Managing Comments* section. Let us examine the functions of the remaining options.

# Managing Posts

As your blog grows, you will need to manage all the posts made by various owners. For this purpose, you can make use of the **All Posts** option. As soon as you click on the link titled **All Posts** from the navigation panel, you will view a new page as shown in the screenshot below:

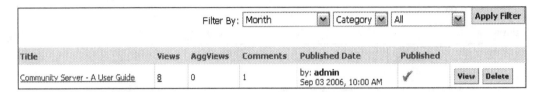

| Title | Views | AggViews | Comments | Published Date | Published | | |
|---|---|---|---|---|---|---|---|
| Community Server - A User Guide | 8 | 0 | 1 | by: **admin**<br>Sep 03 2006, 10:00 AM | ✓ | View | Delete |

You can edit a blog entry by selecting the link located under the **Title** column. You can also view and delete the blog entry using the relevant buttons on the right-hand side. As you will notice from the above screenshot, there are eight views and one comment posted to our sample blog entry. Editing is similar to that when posting a blog except that you will be presented with the content that you have already posted.

You can search the blog entries by using different criteria such as **Month** and also by the various categories. For instance, you can search for only those entries posted on the Forum in the month of June 2006. For our sample blog, we can only see an entry named September 2006 on the **Month** drop-down list because we have just created and started to use the blog. As the site grows, the relevant month and year are automatically added to the list.

You can also search by the publication status of the post. For instance, if there are lot of posts pending for publication in a particular month, you can populate them by selecting the button **Not Published**.

> The search facility is extremely useful as you can quickly view all the posts made on a particular month as your site grows.

# Moderating Blogs and Comments

In the previous sections, we have seen that the relevant blog entry and comments are immediately posted on the site after its submission. In this section, we will examine how to publish the content only after its approval.

Before you approve a post for publication, you should post it to the blog and modify the settings accordingly. For this purpose, click the **My Blogs** link from the top navigation bar inside the **Dashboard** and select **Write a Blog Post** located under the **Common Tasks** panel. Enter the required information to create a new blog post as discussed previously and select the **Save, but don't Publish** button.

We have also chosen to approve all comments submitted for this particular post. For this purpose select the option **All Comments require Approval** from the **Comment Moderation** drop-down list located inside the **Advanced Options** tab.

You can now save the post by clicking on the **Save, but don't Publish** button located at the bottom of the page. As soon as you click on the button, a page as shown in the following screenshot is displayed:

You will notice from the above screenshot that a cross symbol (✖) appears under the **Published** column of the grid. This implies that this post is not published and will not be publicly visible on the site until it is approved by the administrator.

In order to approve the above blog entry, click on the relevant title link from the first row of the grid and click the **Publish** button located at the bottom of the page. You will be returned to the grid and the **Published** column displays a tick symbol ( ✔ ), which signifies that the post has been approved. You can modify the article if you prefer, before its approval. The relevant post will now be visible on the home page of the blog and you can click the link labeled **Current Blog** to view it.

## Approving Comments

Before approving a comment, you should first post a comment by accessing the above blog entry. We have already discussed the usage of comments. However, we will post a sample comment for the purpose of this discussion. As you will observe, the comment will not be visible on the blog page after its submission. This is because we have chosen to moderate it.

In order to approve the comment, you need to select the **Review Comments** link located under the **Common Tasks** navigation panel. You will notice that the comment has not been accepted as the required check mark does not appear under the **Published** column.

In order to approve the comment, click on the **Publish** button. As you may notice, the caption of the button will be changed to **Unpublish**. You can choose whether or not to make a particular comment visible on the site by toggling the button.

Your comment will be immediately approved and will be visible on the relevant blog page.

## Working with Blog Pages

Sometimes, you will need to publish some content that should not appear on the home page of your blog. Instead, you will need to link to that particular content from your blog. It is in this case that the importance of separate blog pages comes into the picture. Community Server includes built-in support for publishing blog pages.

Posting a blog page is very similar to posting a blog entry. The main difference between a post and a blog page is that blog pages are not published to your blog aggregate page (the chronological list of new posts to your blog) as explained above and are also not included in the blog's RSS feed. A blog page is simply an easy way to publish an article or other content, such as a résumé or **About** page, along with your blog. You can include the URL of the relevant blog page while posting a blog entry.

In order to create a blog page, you need to click the **Create a New Page** link from the **Common Tasks** section from the left side navigation bar. Enter the required information and click on the **Publish** button. As soon as you click on the button, the blog page will be created and will be visible inside the grid on the **Blog** pages page as shown in the screenshot below:

 You will be directly taken to the **All Pages** page located under the **Manage Content** navigation panel upon clicking the **Publish** button.

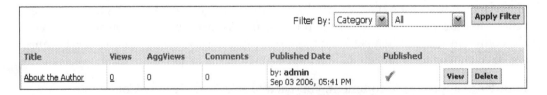

| Title | Views | AggViews | Comments | Published Date | Published | | |
|---|---|---|---|---|---|---|---|
| About the Author | 0 | 0 | 0 | by: **admin**<br>Sep 03 2006, 05:41 PM | ✓ | View | Delete |

You can search for blog pages by the tags created on the site and also by the publication status. You can view a list of all tags created on the site if you pull down the **Category** drop-down list. As you can see from the above screenshot, you can view and delete the blog page by using the relevant buttons.

# Working with Tags

Tags are used to organize the content effectively. The advantage of using tags is that the visitors can easily find the related content as soon as they click on each one of the tags from the home pages of the blogs or forums. You can locate all posts filed under a particular tag quickly. In this section, we will examine the creation of tags and also their usage in detail.

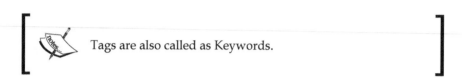

Tags are also called as Keywords.

In order to create a tag, select the **Create New Tag** button by clicking the **Tags/ Keywords** link located under the **Manage Content Panel** located inside the **Blog Management** page. A dialog with the title **Tag Editor** will be displayed. Enter the required name and description as shown in the following screenshot and click on the **Save** button to finish the creation of the new tag.

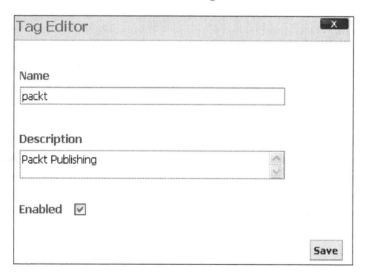

You should also select the **Enabled** checkbox so that the relevant tag will be available while composing or updating a blog or forum post. Otherwise, the tag will not be visible outside the Control Panel.

As soon as the tag is created, it will be displayed on the **Tag/Keywords** grid as shown in the screenshot overleaf:

| Name | Description | Last Post | Posts | Published | Actions |
|------|-------------|-----------|-------|-----------|---------|
| anand | | Sep 03 2006, 05:41 PM | 1 | ✓ | Edit Delete |
| Blogs | | Sep 03 2006, 10:00 AM | 1 | ✓ | Edit Delete |
| CS | | Sep 03 2006, 10:00 AM | 1 | ✓ | Edit Delete |
| File | | Sep 03 2006, 10:00 AM | 1 | ✓ | Edit Delete |
| Forums | | Sep 03 2006, 10:00 AM | 1 | ✓ | Edit Delete |
| Galleries | | Sep 03 2006, 10:00 AM | 1 | ✓ | Edit Delete |
| packt | Packt Publishing | | 0 | ✓ | Edit Delete |
| Photos | | Sep 03 2006, 10:00 AM | 1 | ✓ | Edit Delete |

As you can see, the grid shows a list of all the tags created on the site. The **Last Post** and **Posts** columns on the grid will be updated as and when you file a post using the created tag. You can also modify and delete a tag using the relevant buttons located in the **Actions** column.

> If the tag is not enabled during its creation then the corresponding row on the **Published** grid will display a red X mark.

## Working with Blog Lists

If you maintain a full-fledged blog then you might need to maintain a list of important website, co-workers, or friends' blog addresses and other related URLs in a common place so that you can browse them easily at a later point of time. With Community Server, you can easily post the links under different sections, preferably called **lists**.

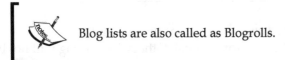

> Blog lists are also called as Blogrolls.

Before beginning to create links, you have to create relevant List under which you will posts these links. From the **Manage Content** section on the left side navigation panel, click on the option titled **All Lists**. Click on the **Create New List** button from the **Blog Lists** page. Enter the required information in the **Link Category**

**Editor** dialog as shown in the next screenshot and click on the **Save** button to create a new list named **Friends:**

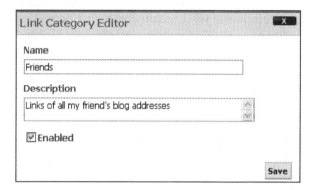

As soon as you click on the **Save** button, the newly created list will be added inside the **Select a List to Manage** drop-down list as shown in the following screenshot:

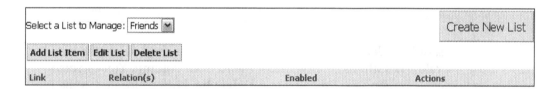

The next step is to create the relevant items under the list named **Friends**. For this purpose, click the **Add List Item** button, enter the required information as shown in the screenshot below, and click on the **Save** button to add the relevant item to the list named **Friends**.

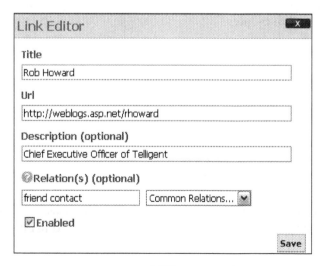

While the **Title** and **URL** fields are compulsory, the **Description** and **Relation(s)** fields are optional. The relations text field will be automatically populated as you select the relevant relation from the **Common Relations** drop-down list. You will have to decide the best relation(s) while adding each list item.

 You can specify more than one relation for a contact and they are separated by spaces.

As soon as you click the **Save** button, the relevant list item will be added inside the grid as shown in the screenshot below:

You have successfully added a new list item. You can modify and delete the list items using the relevant buttons located under the **Actions** column. You can also modify and delete lists using the **Edit List** and **Delete list** buttons located at the top of the grid.

Let us now examine how the list items will appear in our sample blog. Navigate to the home page by clicking on the **Current Blog** link. As soon as you click on the link titled **Links** (see the first screenshot below) located under the heading **This Blog** on the right side of the page, you will be taken to the home page of list items as shown in the second screenshot below:

As you can see from the above screenshot, the list item that we posted is now visible on the site. In the same way, you can create as many lists and list items as per your requirements.

# Working with Snippets

Snippets enable you to quickly create links in your blog posts or pages. This feature is useful if you use a resource found on the Web frequently in your content. When snippets appear in your blog post or page, a link will be automatically generated to the URL that you specified while creating the snippet. Let us now examine how to create a snippet for our sample blog.

Select the link titled **Manage Snippets** from the **Manage Content** navigation panel. Click on the **Create New Snippet** button from the **Manage Blog Snippets** page. Enter the required information as shown in the following screenshot:

As soon as you click the **Save** button, the snippet will be added inside the grid as shown in the screenshot below:

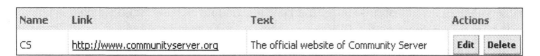

The next step is to properly make use of the above created snippet by creating a new blog post. For this purpose, click on the **Write a Blog Post** link located inside **Common Tasks** panel. In order to use the snippet, you should enclose the snippet name within square brackets. Otherwise, you will not be able to view the effect when you view the blog.

For our sample blog post, we have to supply a text such as **[CS]**, where **CS** is the name of the snippet. It will be replaced with the Text and Link URL that we gave at the time of its creation (see the screenshot titled **Snippet Editor**).

Finally, publish the post and browse to the home page of the blog to view the final output as shown below:

Testing Snippet ★★★★★

The official website of Community Server

Published Monday, September 04, 2006 11:05 PM by <u>admin</u> <u>Edit</u>
[Edit Tags]

## Displaying General Information on the Blog

This option lets you supply description that can start from your career history and then conclude with the launch of the site on your blog. In order to do this, click on the **About My Blog** link located inside the **Manage Content** navigation panel on the **Blog Management** page.

By default, this information will not be displayed on the blog. You can enable it by selecting the **Yes** option from the **Display About My Blog** setting. You should also supply the required title and description in the relevant fields.

Readers of your blog will be taken to the relevant page when they click on the link titled **About** from the home page of the blog.

# Working with Global Settings

In this section, we will examine how to manage some of the general settings of your blog. You should note that any changes to these settings will affect the entire blog.

You will see a lot of options under the heading **Global Settings** located on the left side navigation panel on the **Blog Management** page as shown below:

- **Title, Description, and News**
- **Change how my Blog Looks**
- **My Email Settings**
- **Default Settings for new Posts**
- **Advanced Post Settings**
- **Syndication Settings**
- **Spam, Ping and Cross-Posting Settings**

We will examine each one of the above options in the forthcoming sections of this chapter.

# Supplying Title, Description, and News

You can supply a short title and description of your blog by clicking the **Title, Description, and News** link. The title you enter in the field will be displayed as a link at the top of the page. Clicking the link will enable you to browse the home page of your blog from within the **Blog Management** page.

You can also give brief news about the latest happenings or events which may occur to your blog. This is an optional setting and the information entered in the news field will be displayed on the right side of the home page of the blog as a separate section as shown in the following screenshot:

It is also possible to give the required meta tags for all the pages by using **Search meta Description** and **Search meta Keywords** fields. The information you enter in these fields will be displayed when a user performs a search on the Web using search engines. The keywords should preferably be separated by commas.

# Changing the Appearance of your Blog

You can modify the look and feel of your blog by using various themes included with Community Server. Themes will change the entire behavior of your blog including the placement of links by making use of **Cascading Style Sheets (CSS)**. In order to modify the appearance of your blog, click the **Change How My Blog Looks** link from the left side navigation panel.

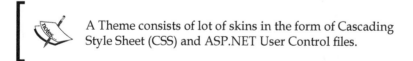

As you can see, the **Theme** drop-down list displays lot of themes under various names. You should select any one of them for your blog. As soon as you select a theme, its preview will be displayed at the bottom as shown in the screenshot overleaf. This will help you to select another one, if the theme you selected doesn't meet your expectations.

Modifying a theme using this option will only affect the current active blog. If you need to modify themes for other blogs, then you should switch blogs by using the **Select Blog to Manage** button located on the extreme right-hand side. You can globally specify a theme for all the blogs on the site from the blogs section by selecting the **Administration** link from the **Dashboard**.

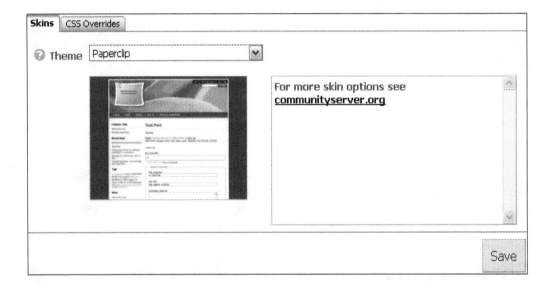

Click on the **Save** button after selecting a theme. If you now browse the home page of this blog by clicking on the **Current Blog** link at the top of the page you will be able to see that the appearance of your blog has been completely changed.

 Several customization packs are available from the **Downloads** section at http://www.communityserver. org. These packs include additional themes for your blog, which you can use to further enhance the appearance of your blog.

# Configuring Email Settings

You can specify your email address and enable related options by clicking the **My Email Settings** link. First, you should specify an email address in the **Blog contact email address** field, where you wish to receive all communications submitted through the contact form on the blog. But you should also select the **Enable Contact Me** option in order to receive those email messages. The email address will not be shared or published. However, you can choose to share the email address by replying to a message that you receive from the site.

The final setting on the page, **Email Notifications**, enables you to disable the delivery of email notifications for those comments posted on the site that are rated as spam messages. Sometimes, visitors to your blog will post unnecessary comments. Community Server automatically isolates those comments as spam. If you enable this setting then the user who posts spam messages will not receive an email from the system.

# Working with Post Settings

You can modify the settings associated with some of the core functionalities such as comment moderation, rating, and the display of content on your home page by clicking the **Default Post Settings** link. We will examine each one of the settings in detail.

## Allow Comments on my blog

If this is enabled, visitors can post comments to your blog posts. By default, comments are enabled. This option applies to all blogs, while the same option covered under the *Writing Your Blog Entry* section applies only to that particular entry and overrides this default.

## Comment Moderation

You can specify how to publish comments on the blog. By default, all comments are published immediately. But if you prefer, you can choose to approve the comments before their publication. You should make sure to choose the appropriate option from the drop-down list before attempting to publish a blog post. Otherwise, comments will be posted even if you enable comment moderation individually while posting the blog posts.

## Send me email notifications

You can specify whether you should receive email notifications for the feedback submissions and comments posted on the site. By default, you will not receive any email from the visitors. For instance, if you choose **All Comments** from the list then you will receive email notifications for all the comments posted on the site.

### Allow readers to rate posts

If set to yes, registered members can rate all blog posts on a scale of 1 to 5. We will examine ratings in detail later on in this chapter.

### Allow tracking of external references to my posts (trackbacks)

If this is enabled, trackbacks or pingbacks will be made on all outgoing links. But these will be sent only when the post is published for the first time. They are not sent out when you edit a blog post.

### New posts are displayed on my blog's homepage

If this is enabled, all new posts will be displayed on the homepage of your blog. The relevant blog posts will also be included on the main syndication feeds.

### New posts are displayed on this site's homepage

If this is enabled, all new posts will be displayed on the homepage of your site.

### Publish post excerpts when my content is syndicated (RSS)

If this is enabled, the excerpt that you entered while writing a post will be syndicated instead of the entire post. By default, this setting is disabled.

### Auto Name Posts

If this is enabled, Community Server will name your posts based on the title that you entered for the blog in the **Title**, **Description**, and **News** page. This setting is enabled by default. The title will appear on top of each blog post.

# Understanding Blog-Level Settings

In order to access blog-level settings, you should click the **Advanced Post Settings** link from the navigation panel on the left side. You should note that any modification to these settings will affect all existing and new blog posts. Let us examine each one of the settings in detail:

### Allow Anonymous Users to Comment

If this is enabled, anonymous users can post comments to your blog posts. Anonymous users are those who are not logged into the site. This setting is disabled by default.

### Comment Moderation

The function of this setting has been discussed in the *Working with Post Settings* section. The only difference is that you have the option to **Ignore** comments if you use the setting on this page.

### Allow Comments on my blog

The function of this setting has already been discussed in the *Working with Post Settings* section.

### Allow tracking of external references to my posts (trackbacks)

The function of this setting has already been discussed in the *Working with Post Settings* section.

### Comment Day Limits

You can specify the number of days for which you wish to allow comments for the new posts. When the specified number of days expires, new comments will not be accepted. For instance, if you set the value to 30 days then your visitors can post their comments for the first 30 days from the date of posting of the blog entry.

### Allow readers to rate posts

The function of this setting has already been discussed in the *Working with Post Settings* section.

# Understanding Syndication using RSS & Atom

Syndication is a new concept introduced when blogs became popular among the community. With syndication, your blog posts are transformed into industry-standard XML formats and other websites can display them if used correctly. Simply speaking, you can aggregate all blog posts made under each blog to a single location. In order to enable or disable the relevant settings, click on the **Syndication Settings** link from the navigation panel on the left-hand side. Let us now examine each one of the settings in detail:

### Enable RSS Syndication

If this is enabled, the blog will generate a, RSS feed, which will be read by RSS or feed readers.

### Enable RSS Comments

If this is enabled, comments can be posted directly to the relevant blog entry by using RSS readers. You should set **Enable RSS Comments** to true in order to take advantage of this feature.

### Enable RSS for Tags

If this is enabled, an RSS hyperlink will be displayed on the search result page while performing a search on the site with tags as shown in the following screenshot:

Browse by Tags
All Tags » CS (RSS)

Blogs  File  Forums  Galleries  Photos

## Community Server - A User Guide

In this book, you will learn how to create and manage Blogs, Forums, Galleries, Downloads using the latest version of Community Server. In addition, you will also learn how to customize and deploy the application. Read More...

Posted Sunday, September 03, 2006 6:00 PM by admin | 1 Comments [Edit]
Filed under: Galleries, CS, Photos, Blogs, Forums, File [Edit Tags]

Attachment(s): PacktLogoSmall.png

## Enable Atom Syndication

If this is enabled, the blog will generate an Atom feed that can be read by RSS readers. Some readers will support only Atom but some will support both RSS and Atom.

Atom is an alternative format to RSS. You will find more details about Atom at:
`http://en.wikipedia.org/wiki/Atom_(standard)`

## Syndicate External Links

If this is enabled, all the external links that you post on the blog entries will be syndicated and feed readers will be able to read them.

By default, the settings **Enable RSS Syndication**, **Enable RSS for Tags**, and **Enable Atom Syndication** are enabled.

From the **External Feed URL** section you can specify the complete URL of your blog feed if you use an external syndication service.

# Working with Spam, Ping, and Cross-Posting Settings

Community Server provides a system for site administrators to specify spam and ping settings. Clicking the **Spam, Ping and Cross-Posting** link, will display a page with three options.

The first option enables you to specify custom spam scores. This is a blog-level setting and will affect only the current active blog and will override the related score set for the site. You can specify scores for flagging comments for moderation and also for automatically deleting comments that are recognized as spam.

With the help of the second option, you can specify the URLs of all the services that should be pinged while adding or modifying a blog post. You can include any number of URLs separated by semicolons.

The final option enables you to specify cross-posting settings, but this feature has been disabled by default. Refer to the *Enable Cross-Posting* section of the *Managing Blogs Globally* section below for more information regarding this setting.

# Rating Blog Posts

Rating enables you to give credit to a blog post or an article. For instance, you can give a 5 star rating for a high quality post or article. You can give a lower rating if you feel that the post or article doesn't meet your expectations. With Community Server, you can rate a post very easily.

In order to rate a blog post, log in as an administrator or as a user and from the home page navigate to a blog post for which you wish to give rating. You will now see a small rectangle with 5 stars as shown in the next screenshot:

About Chapter 3 ☆☆☆☆☆

In chapter 3, we will examine the working of Blogs

Published Monday, September 04, 2006 12:24 AM by <u>admin</u> <u>Edit</u>
<u>[Edit Tags]</u>

If you point the mouse cursor over the stars, its colour will change as shown in the following screenshot. You will also be able to see a tool tip as shown in the screenshot if you point the mouse cursor over each star.

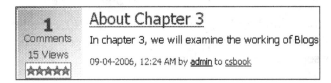

You need to click on the relevant star in order to rate a blog post. The stars will blink for a while after you click on them. When the blinking stops, the post will be rated and the rating stars will appear on the home page of the blog alongside the post heading as shown in the next screenshot:

| 1 | About Chapter 3 |
|---|---|
| Comments | In chapter 3, we will examine the working of Blogs |
| 15 Views | 09-04-2006, 12:24 AM by admin to csbook |
| ★★★★★ | |

# Managing Blogs Globally

As a site administrator, you can specify permissions and other related settings for the management and appearance of blogs globally. In this section, we will examine these options in detail.

Firstly, you should log in as an administrator and open the **Dashboard** by clicking on the **Control Panel** link located at the top of the page. Once you are inside the **Dashboard** click on the link titled **Administration**. You will see a new page with the caption **Site Administration**. From the page, you can give permissions for various applications included with Community Server. You should note that any modification to any of the settings will affect the whole site globally.

Pull down the **Blogs** link from the navigation panel located on the left side. You will see a series of options. We have already examined the first three options in the earlier sections of this chapter. Let us examine the other options.

The **Global Permissions** option enables you to specify various permissions globally. You can, however, modify them individually for each blog at the time of its creation.

The **Default Settings** option includes several settings for the management of blogs. We will examine each one of them in detail:

## Create Directories

If this is enabled, a new directory will be created for each new blog. The advantage of this feature is that you can access the blog without specifying `default.aspx` at the end of the URL. This setting is enabled by default.

## Auto Create

If this is enabled, a new blog will be automatically created when a new user registers on the site.

## Enable Cross-Posting

If this is enabled, the blog owners can cross-post all the entries to one or more remote blogs by taking advantage of the **metaWeblog Application Programming Interface**. This feature is disabled by default. If you enable it then you can set up remote blogs by clicking the **Spam, Ping and Cross-Posting** link located under the **Global Settings** section inside your Blog Management area. You will be asked to give the required username, password, and other related settings. Whenever you post a blog entry from your Community Server site, it will be also posted to the specified remote blog provided, if the settings given are correct.

## Enable Blog Owners to add content to HTML Head

If this is enabled, blog owners can add raw content such as meta tags and JavaScript to their blog pages inside the **Head** tag.

## Default Group

You can specify a default blog group using this setting. All new blogs will be added to this group.

## Default Ping Services

You can include the URLs that Community Server should ping while adding or modifying a blog post. By default four URLs are included, but you can add more if required. Each URL should be separated by semicolons.

## Default Aggregate Tags

With the help of this setting, you can specify a list of tags that will be included on the home page of the blog and on the RSS feeds, by default. These tags will be visible to all blog owners.

## Service Post Count Limit

This setting enables you to specify the maximum number of posts that should be returned by the Community Server web services such as CS Weblog and metaWeblog services.

The **Default Presentation** option enables you to specify the settings related to appearance of the blog and blog posts.

### Enable Themes

You can enable themes using this setting. The blog owners will be able to choose one of the themes from the provided list, which will ultimately change the look and feel of their blog. This setting is enabled by default.

### Default Theme

You can select a theme that will be used for all new blogs created on the site by default. However, blog owners can change it from the **Blog Management** page.

### Aggregate Post Count

You can specify the maximum number of posts that should be displayed on the aggregate home page of the blog on the site. The page can be accessed by clicking the **Blogs** link from the home page of the site. The default value for this setting is 25. Hence, the first 25 posts will be visible on the home page and the remaining posts will be automatically paginated.

### Individual Blog Post Count

You can specify the maximum number of posts that should be displayed on the home page of the individual blog. The default value for this setting is 15. Hence, the first 15 posts will be visible on the home page and the remaining posts will be automatically paginated.

### Service Post Count Limit

You can specify the maximum number of posts that should be displayed by the CS web services such as CS Weblog and metaWeblog services. The default value for this setting is 25. Hence, the first 25 posts will be visible on the home page and the remaining posts will be automatically paginated.

### Aggregate Post Excerpt Size

With the help of this setting, you can specify the maximum number of characters for each post that should be displayed on the aggregate home page of the community. The default value for this setting is 250.

The **Enable Post Relevance Sorting** setting inside the **Post Relevance Sorting** section enables you to specify the settings related to the relevance of blog posts. Community Server considers the various factors, using which your posts are sorted and displayed on the site. The advantage of this setting is that the popular posts appear on the home page much longer than those posts with less importance. The blog home page always displays posts with high importance. This setting is disabled by default.

# Configuring Blogs for Members

We have so far examined the creation and management of blogs as an administrator. Let us now discuss how to configure a blog for a registered member on the site. We assume that you are the site administrator. This is the kind of job that you will likely implement if your site is especially oriented for a big community.

For example, msmvps.com is a site that provides separate blogs for every Microsoft Most Valuable Professional. The site is of course maintained by one administrator, but a lot of MVPs, including the author of this book, have separate blog accounts on the site.

To configure a blog for a registered member, you will have to follow certain basic steps as outlined below

1. Ask the member to register on the site.
2. Get the username from that specific member for whom you wish to create a blog.
3. Log in as an administrator, create a new blog and give ownership rights to that specific member.
4. Inform the member about the URL of the blog.

 Refer to the section *Creating a Blog* for more information regarding blog creation.

Once the above-mentioned steps are completed then the specific member to whom you gave access to manage the blog can log in to the site and begin to work on their blog.

 The registered member should log in to the site by using the URL to manage the blog.

Initially, the blog home page will not display any content or the relevant links for managing the blog (see the next screenshot). However, members can view the blog entries of the entire site by selecting **Entire Site** from the search section located at the top of the page.

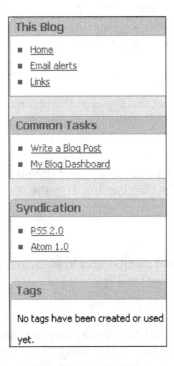

But as soon as a member logs in the above panel will display the relevant links for managing the blog as shown in the screenshot below:

If you compare the two screenshots displayed opposite, you can see that a new section with the title **Common Tasks** has appeared after the member has logged into the site.

The owner of the blog should click the link titled **Write a Blog Post** to compose a new blog entry and **My Blog Dashboard** to navigate to the **Blog Management** page of the **Control Panel** (see screenshot below).

As you can see from the above screenshot, the user interface looks very similar to the set of links that we examined earlier. The **Current Blog** section displays a link with the title of the blog being maintained by the member and not that of our sample blog. The only notable difference is that the owner will have control over only their blog and not others. For instance, if the specific owner navigates to the **All Posts** area inside the **Manage Content** section, they will not be able to view the blog entries posted by all blog owners. The relevant posts will appear as and when the owner of the blog submits content in the form of posts and blog pages. Moreover, the **Blog Author(s) and General Statistics** of the **My Blog Dashboard** will be updated as soon as the owner begins to work on the blog.

If the site administrator creates another blog for the same owner then it will also appear inside the blog **Dashboard** and it can be viewed if the blog owner clicks the **Select Blog to Manage** button located at the top of the page.

# Summary

Blogs are a simple and easy way to allow people to publish ideas, thoughts, or feedback. Community Server provides a complete blogging platform that helps users set up and use blogs effectively. This chapter helped you to understand all the essential theories behind the blog application shipped with Community Server. We thoroughly examined all the key aspects associated with blogs such as creation of tags, snippets, and lists, syndication, and rating with a help of a sample blog. Towards the end, we also examined how to configure and set up a blog for a registered member. The next chapter will explain how to create and manage forums using Community Server.

# 4
# Working with Forums

In the previous chapter, we examined the creation and management of blogs. In this chapter, we will examine another Community Server application, **forums**. You will learn how to create, manage, and administer discussion forums. Towards the end of this chapter, we will investigate the home page of forums from the points of view of an Administrator and User, and also the aspects involved with personalization of the forum home page.

## A Brief History of Forums

An effective communication channel is a must for any individual or business to succeed. Even though there are numerous ways such as letters, email, and telephone, they are restricted to the people who are communicating. This means that other individuals can't benefit from their conversation. Web-based discussion forums allow conversations to be shared among a group of people and archived for future participants.

Forums play a very crucial role in our day-to-day life where communication via technology is involved. They are used as a standard communication tool for small groups, organizations, and large businesses. Each and every kind of business has its own forums on their website. For instance, a web hosting company can host a forum on its website to provide support and assistance for its customers. In a similar way, a medical professional can host a forum to provide assistance and also to create awareness about various types of diseases, treatments, and other health-related issues.

With web discussions not only can end users post their questions for expert opinion but other users also can get benefit from the previous postings. Sometimes, a solution that one user has been looking for might have already been provided by another user and this reduces the time required for disposal of issues. It is difficult to develop fully fledged forum software within a few days. It requires a huge effort of a large number of developers. It is in this situation that the importance of ready-made forum-development software comes into the picture. Many companies have released forum applications using various technologies such as PHP, ASP, and ASP.NET over the last several years. PHP-based forums were the first to be introduced followed by ASP and ASP.NET.

ASP.NET-based forums are becoming more popular because of the unique simplicity and customization capabilities of ASP.NET. Forums are managed with the help of a database, which will run in the background. While PHP-based forums make use of a MySQL database, ASP, and ASP.NET based products use either Microsoft Access, or SQL Server 2000, or SQL Server 2005. Community Server includes a powerful built-in forums application as shown in the screenshot below:

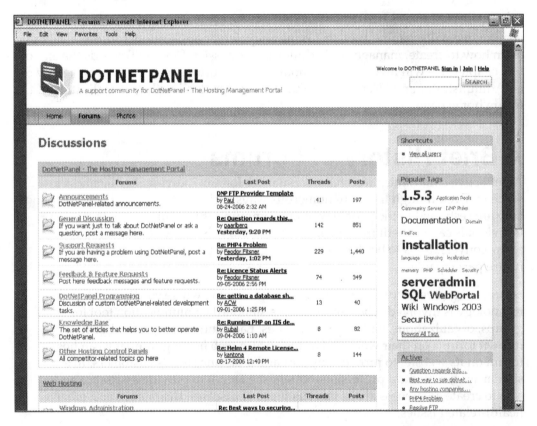

You can also see forums powered with Community Server live at several websites such as `http://communityserver.org/forums/default.aspx`, `http://forums.xbox.com`, `http://forums.asp.net`, and `http://www.aspnix.com/forums/default.aspx`. You can either deploy them as a single standalone application or they can run as integrated solutions along with other Community Server applications such as blogs and photo galleries. Forums do not require separate installation as they are a part of Community Server. You will learn about the creation and management of forums in the forthcoming sections of this chapter.

# Getting Started: A Sample Forum

We will demonstrate the concepts with the help of a sample forum meant for developers. After the creation of the forum, you will be able to post and reply queries regarding various programming languages and technologies used by the majority of developers.

Before proceeding further you should log in to the Community Server as a user with administration privileges. This can be done by visiting the home page and signing in using the Administrator username and password you configured during installation.

As with blogs, forums also have a separate home page. For our sample forum, its web address will look like `http://localhost/cs21/forums/default.aspx`. The initial home page from the point of view of an Administrator will appear as shown below:

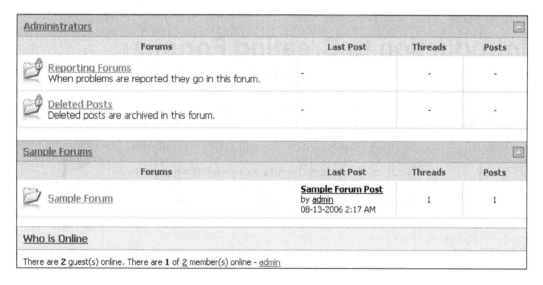

The page shown above will look similar for other users when they visit this page as they will be shown a list of forum groups. However, the list of forums may not be the same, as it depends upon the user's permission levels. Forums support private forums, controlled by permissions, and in the screenshot above you can see forums only available to a site Administrator. Let us now examine each section of the default home page of the forum in detail.

By default, the installer creates two forums: **Reporting Forums** and **Deleted Posts**. These forums are solely meant for Administrators and will not be visible for end users.

**Reporting Forums**: If users report problems with posts from other forums, their messages will show up in **Reporting Forums**.

**Deleted Posts**: When posts are deleted they are moved to this forum. The **Deleted Posts** forum is similar to the Windows recycle bin.

In the screenshot on the previous page you can see that the home page displays the total number of registered members and guests who are currently online. Guests are anonymous people that are browsing but have not signed in. The **Forum Statistics** section will show how many users have contributed to the forums, the number of threads posted, and the newest member.

 In forums parlance, a **thread** is a group of related messages.

# Introduction to Creating Forums

In order to create a forum, click on the **Control Panel** link from the top navigation bar of the home page. You will see a new page with the title **Dashboard**. Here click on the link titled **Add new forums, control permissions, etc.** located under the heading **Forums Administration** to navigate to the **Site Administration** page.

 You can also access the **Site Administration** page by clicking on the **Control Panel** link and then selecting the **Administration** link from the navigation bar located at the top of the page.

You will now see a set of six links under the heading **Forums** as shown below:

Before creating the required forums on the site, you should first create relevant forum groups, so that you can file each forum under the appropriate group. Let us examine how to create the required groups for our sample forum.

# Creating Forum Groups

In order to create forum groups, click on the link titled **Forum Groups** from the **Forums** navigation panel. You can see that two new groups with the name **Administrators** and **Sample Forums** have been automatically created after installation.

For our sample forum, we will create two groups with the name Microsoft and Non-Microsoft. To create these groups, click on the **New Group** button and enter the required information as shown in the screenshot below:

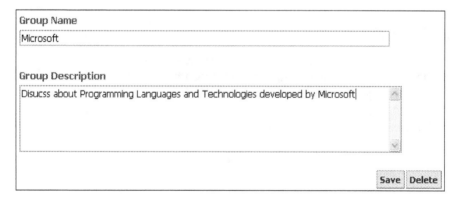

The **Group Description** can be of any length but it is a recommended practice to restrict it to one or two sentences for the sake of clarity. Clicking the **Save** button located at the bottom of the page will add the group to the grid displaying forum groups. In the same way, create another group called Non-Microsoft by supplying the required information as explained above.

After the creation of groups, the grid inside the forum groups page will appear as shown in the next screenshot.

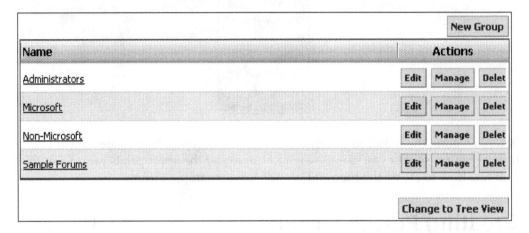

You can edit the group name and description by selecting the **Edit** button. You can directly manage the relevant forums filed under a specific group by clicking the **Manage** button from the appropriate row. For simplicity, you can also modify the look and feel of the page to tree-view format, if you prefer.

We have now created the forum groups required for our sample forum. Let us now examine the creation of forums.

## Creating Forums

In order to create the required forums, click on the **Create New Forum** link in the **Forums** section from the navigation panel located on the left side of the **Site Administration** page. You will view a page with four tabs: **Basic**, **Advanced**, **User Permissions**, and **Admin Permissions** as shown in the following screenshot. You need to first enter the required information such as a name for the forum, description, etc. using the **Basic** and **Advanced** tabs. You should also specify permissions using the **User** and **Admin Permissions** tabs.

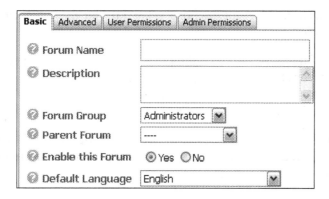

We will now create the required forums for our group **Microsoft**. For this purpose, we will create a new forum with the name ASP. We will supply a short description such as "Discuss Classic ASP here" for our forum.

Let's look at the tabs in detail.

## Basic

The **Basic** tab provides options necessary for creating a forum that are described below:

**Forum Name**: You should specify the name of the forum (e.g. ASP).

**Description**: You should describe the forum in few lines.

**Forum Group**: You should specify, appropriate Group Name from the options available in the drop-down box (e.g. Microsoft).

**Parent Forum**: You should specify a parent forum from the drop-down box that will contain this forum as subforum.

**Enable this Forum**: By default, the forum that we created is enabled. If required you can select **No** and then enable it when you are ready to launch the forum. If disabled, the forum will not be visible outside Administrator's control panel.

**Default Language**: You should select the desired language from the drop-down box.

## Advanced

The **Advanced** tab provides facilities to perform some of the other tasks associated with forums as described below:

**URL**: You should specify a URL if you wish to use the forum that you created as a tracked link.

**Index Posts**: If this is enabled, all the posts posted under the specific forum are indexed for searching.

**Moderate Posts**: If this is enabled, all the posts posted under the specific forum require approval from the concerned person or moderator before publication on the forum. A moderator can either be an Administrator or any other person approved by the Administrator. By default, this feature is disabled.

**Enable Post Statistics**: If this is enabled, the posts are counted and displayed below the Username of each user. This enables an Administrator to determine how many posts a specific user has contributed to the Forum.

**Enable Post Points**: If this is enabled, the posts are given points and the relevant points are displayed below the Username of each user.

**Enable Post Auto-Delete**: If this is enabled, the posts are automatically deleted after a specified interval.

**Auto-Delete Time Window**: This denotes the number of days after which the posts should be automatically deleted from the specific forum. By default, it is 90 days from the date of posting.

## User Permissions

This tab is used to grant permissions to the users accessing the forum. All registered users, by default, will have the authority to perform all tasks such as viewing, editing of posts, etc.

## Admin Permissions

An Administrator can grant the desired permissions to users, moderators, and others using this tab. For our sample forum, we will keep all these settings as such without any modifications.

 You can globally give permissions for all the active forums from the **Global Permissions** link located on the left navigation panel under the heading **Forums**.

Finally, click on the **Save** button to create our new forum named **ASP**. As soon as the forum is created, you will be taken to the **Forums** page where you will see a list of all the forums that have been created on the site, including the default forum created by the installer.

In the similar way, we will create other forums with the names **ASP.NET 1.1, ASP. NET 2.0**, and **Visual Basic .NET** under the **Microsoft** Group. We will also create four forums named **PHP**, **PERL**, **Java**, and **Python** under the **Non-Microsoft** group. We have now successfully created the required forums under two different groups. The forums grid after the creation of all forums will appear as shown in the screenshot below:

| Name | Description | Group | Enabled | Actions |
|------|-------------|-------|---------|---------|
| Reporting Forums | When problems are reported they go in this forum. | Administrators | ✓ | Edit View Delete |
| Deleted Posts | Deleted posts are archived in this forum. | Administrators | ✓ | Edit View Delete |
| ASP | Discuss Classic ASP. | Microsoft | ✓ | Edit View Delete |
| ASP.NET 1.1 | Discuss ASP.NET 1.1 here. | Microsoft | ✓ | Edit View Delete |
| ASP.NET 2.0 | Discuss ASP.NET 2.0 here. | Microsoft | ✓ | Edit View Delete |
| Visual Basic .NET | Discuss Visual Basic .NET here. | Microsoft | ✓ | Edit View Delete |
| PHP | Discuss PHP. (all versions) | Non-Microsoft | ✓ | Edit View Delete |
| PERL | Discuss PERL language here. | Non-Microsoft | ✓ | Edit View Delete |
| Java | Discuss Java programming language here. | Non-Microsoft | ✓ | Edit View Delete |
| Python | Discuss Python language here. | Non-Microsoft | ✓ | Edit View Delete |

Group: All Forum Groups

You can display the forums based on each group using the **Group** drop-down box located on the right side of the page as shown in the above screenshot. For instance, if you select **Microsoft**, the grid will display only those forums created under that group as shown below:

Group: Microsoft

| Name | Description | Group | Enabled | Actions |
|------|-------------|-------|---------|---------|
| ASP | Discuss Classic ASP. | Microsoft | ✓ | Edit View Delete |
| ASP.NET 1.1 | Discuss ASP.NET 1.1 here. | Microsoft | ✓ | Edit View Delete |
| ASP.NET 2.0 | Discuss ASP.NET 2.0 here. | Microsoft | ✓ | Edit View Delete |
| Visual Basic .NET | Discuss Visual Basic .NET here. | Microsoft | ✓ | Edit View Delete |

As you can observe from the above screenshot, displaying forums based on group name will not only reduce the space but also help you to easily locate and manage the forums.

# Viewing Sample Forums

In the previous section, we have seen how to create forums under two different groups. Let us now examine how to view the finished home page of our sample forum.

Click on the link titled **Exit Control Panel and Return to Site** located in the top section of the **Site Administration** page to return to the home page of our site. Select the **Forums** link from the top navigation bar to visit to the home page of our forum as shown in the following screenshot. You should note that you are currently logged in as an Administrator and the home page is meant for Administrators.

| Administrators | | | |
|---|---|---|---|
| **Forums** | **Last Post** | **Threads** | **Posts** |
| **Reporting Forums**<br>When problems are reported they go in this forum | - | - | - |
| **Deleted Posts**<br>Deleted posts are archived in this forum. | - | - | - |

| Sample Forums | | | |
|---|---|---|---|
| **Forums** | **Last Post** | **Threads** | **Posts** |
| **Sample Forum** | **Sample Forum Post**<br>by admin<br>08-13-2006 2:17 AM | 1 | 1 |

| Microsoft | | | |
|---|---|---|---|
| **Forums** | **Last Post** | **Threads** | **Posts** |
| **ASP**<br>Discuss about Classic ASP here. | - | - | - |
| **ASP.NET 1.1**<br>Discuss about ASP.NET 1.1 here. | - | - | - |
| **ASP.NET 2.0**<br>Discuss about ASP.NET 2.0 here. | - | - | - |
| **Visual Basic .NET**<br>Discuss about Visual Basic .NET here. | - | - | - |

| Non-Microsoft | | | |
|---|---|---|---|
| **Forums** | **Last Post** | **Threads** | **Posts** |
| **PHP**<br>Discuss about PHP here. (All Versions) | - | - | - |
| **PERL**<br>Discuss about PERL here. | - | - | - |

You can also see a forum post under the forum **Sample Forums**. As noted earlier, this forum was automatically created at the time of installation of Community Server.

# Posting a Thread as an Administrator

Let us now discuss how to post a thread to one of our sample forums — ASP. NET 2.0. We assume that you are logged in as an Administrator. Navigate to the home page by clicking on the **Forums** link from the navigation bar and select the appropriate forum. Initially, you will view a page as shown below:

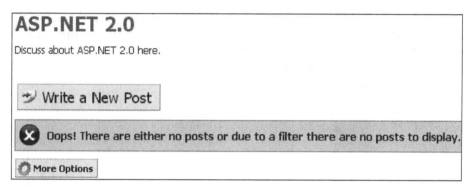

You can sort the posts under the specific forum using different criteria found under the **Sorting and Notifications** panel by clicking the **More Options** button. In addition to this, you can also choose an option for notification. Community Server will automatically deliver an email to the logged in user whenever new posts are posted to the relevant forum. The panel also shows the various features and permissions that are available for the specific forum.

Click on the **Write a New Post** button to post a new thread. You will now see a new page, which contains a text editor with six tabs as shown below.

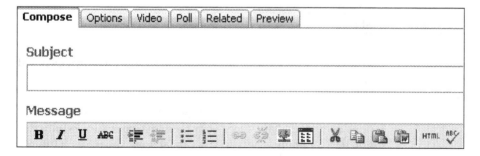

By default, a standard text editor with a limited set of options as shown overleaf is displayed. You can, however, modify the setting to display an advanced text editor with rich features such as ability to change fonts and sizes, insert emoticons, and so on.

 Emoticons are not enabled by default. You have to enable them from the **Post Settings** page located under the **Settings** panel from the **Site Administration** page.

The settings can be modified by logging to the site and selecting the username displayed as a link at the top of the home page. Select the **Site Options** tab and modify the value of the **Content Editor** drop-down list from **Standard** to **Enhanced** and click the **Save Changes** button. You will see a new text editor with a new interface as shown below:

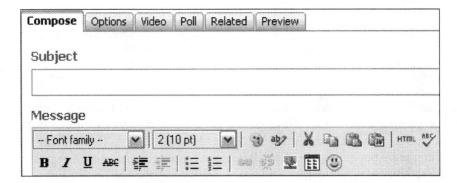

## Compose

In order to write a new post, you need to enter the required subject and the content for the message in the appropriate fields as shown below:

| Field Name | Test Data |
| --- | --- |
| Subject | What are the new features of ASP.NET 2.0? |
| Message | Can anybody post information regarding the new features included with ASP.NET 2.0? |
| Tag | You can also enter the required tags separated by commas, which will be displayed on the bottom of each post. You can later on browse the forums using these tags. Once your tags have been successfully stored inside the Community Server, you can later use them for all future posts by selecting the **Select Tags** button. |

You can format the message using the options available in the text editor. For our sample post, we will modify the font and size of the message. You can also insert emoticons if you wish to display them. But before posting the message, we will explore the additional features associated with posts.

## Options

You can manage attachments, sticky posts, etc. by selecting the **Options** tab while posting a new thread.

**File Attachment**: You can upload a file, which will be added as an attachment to your message. A pop-up dialog will be displayed when you click on the **Add/Update** button in the **Options** tab. You can either upload a file from your local system or specify a web address where the required file is located.

**Do not allow replies**: If this is enabled, members cannot post replies to threads. By default, this option is disabled.

**Stickiness**: You can post a thread that will always remain visible for a fixed period of days as specified by the Administrator while posting the thread. By default, posts are not set as sticky.

**Post Icon**: You can pick any one of the smilies from the available list, which will be displayed as a first item on the subject line of the corresponding forum. These icons reflect the nature of the posts.

 Only Administrators can post a Sticky thread.

## Video

You can post videos by using the options available on the **Video** tab that are described below:

**Video URL**: You can specify a URL where the relevant video is located.

**Preview Image URL**: You can specify a URL where the preview image is located.

**Video Duration**: You can specify the duration of the video.

**Video Width**: You can specify the width of the video.

**Video Height**: You can specify the height of the video.

## Poll

You can convert a regular post into a poll by selecting the **Include a Poll in this Post** option from the **Poll** tab. An important point to note is that you have to control the placement of polls on the message by placing the *[Poll]* tag appropriately.

## Related

In addition to the above features, you can also view only those messages that relate to or closely match the current post.

## Preview

You can also sneak a preview of the post before it is posted to the forum so that you can perform any changes if required.

# Posting the Message to the Forum

As soon as you click on the **Post** button, the message will be added to the relevant forum as shown below:

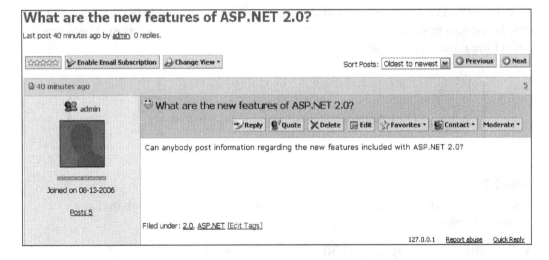

From the above screenshot, you can observe that the message has been posted by a user with the username **admin**. Moreover, the admin has made a total number of five posts. The posts made on the blogs also count towards the total. The page also mentions the date on which the user joined the site. As noted earlier, the page also displays the tags used for posting this message under the section **Filed Under**. These tags will be available when you submit another post later on.

Members can rate the post and also activate email subscription. If this feature is enabled, members will receive an email as and when a new post has been posted on this thread. You can also change the view to **Flat View** or **Threaded View** using the **Change View** drop-down list.

On the right-hand side, you will see a series of buttons, which are used for various purposes while working with the relevant post. Let us now explore them in detail.

## Replying to a Post

In order to reply to a post, members should click the **Reply** button from the relevant post. The **Subject** field will be automatically populated with the original title. You should enter the required content in the **Message** field as shown in the following screenshot. You can also select the required tags by selecting the **Select Tags** button at the bottom of the page, which is displayed below:

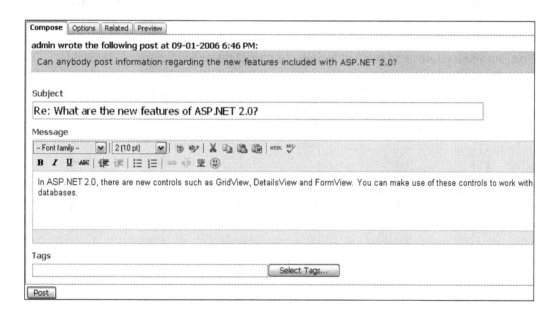

As soon as you click the **Post** button, the reply will be displayed as a fresh post below the original post. You should note that the **Post** icon will not be visible on the reply unless you specify it again from the **Options** tab.

## Replying to a Post with a Quote

In order to reply to a post with the original post as a quote, members should click the **Quote** button from the relevant post. As soon as you click on the button, a page as shown in the following screenshot is displayed:

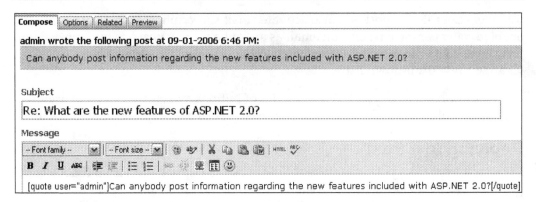

As you can see, a new tag has been added before and after the message content. The reply will be posted along with the original post content. This will help users to quickly track the subject being discussed especially if the thread spans several pages.

## Deleting a Post

You can remove a thread or post by selecting the **Delete** button. For instance, if you attempt to delete your sample post, a new page will be displayed as shown in the screenshot opposite, which will prompt you to enter a reason for deletion. The reason will be logged and the original author of the post will receive an email with a message that his/her post has been deleted.

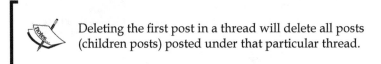

Deleting the first post in a thread will delete all posts (children posts) posted under that particular thread.

You should note that only Administrators or moderators are able to delete a thread or post.

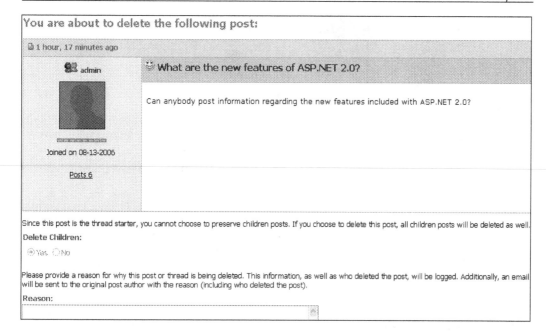

You are about to delete the following post:

🗎 1 hour, 17 minutes ago

👤 admin

😊 What are the new features of ASP.NET 2.0?

Can anybody post information regarding the new features included with ASP.NET 2.0?

Joined on 08-13-2006

Posts 6

Since this post is the thread starter, you cannot choose to preserve children posts. If you choose to delete this post, all children posts will be deleted as well.

**Delete Children:**

⦿Yes ○No

Please provide a reason for why this post or thread is being deleted. This information, as well as who deleted the post, will be logged. Additionally, an email will be sent to the original post author with the reason (including who deleted the post).

**Reason:**

## Editing a Post

In order to modify the content of a post, you should click the **Edit** button. The interface looks similar to the one used for posting a message. The only difference is that you will find two text fields with the named as **Edit Notes** and **Current Edit Notes** at the bottom of the text editor. Even if you submit the form without adding any information to these fields, Community Server automatically inserts **Edit Notes**. You should note that an **Edit Note** once added cannot be modified. You can also pick some tags by selecting the **Select Tags** button.

The **Current Edit Notes** field is read only.

The **Edit Notes** text field will not appear on the relevant message page and will be visible only to the Administrator or the relevant member upon editing the message.

## Working with Favorites

In order to use the Favorites feature, you should first select **Favorites** button. Clicking on the drop-down arrow will display a list of three options as shown on the next page.

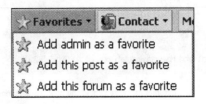

The main purpose of this feature is to increase the points for the relevant user, post, or forum that is added as a favorite. You can choose an option according to your preference but you should note that adding a user, post, or forum as a favorite affects the member points score for that particular user, post, or forum.

For more information regarding member points, refer to Chapter 11 — *Working with System Tools*.

## Managing Contacts

In order to interact with the member who posted the message, you need to click the **Contact** button. Clicking on the drop-down arrow will display a list of options as shown below:

From the above screenshot, you will notice that the message has been posted by a member with the username **admin**. With the help of this feature, members can send an email or a private message to the member who posted the message. It is also possible to view the members's profile and also search for all posts posted by a particular member.

As the name suggests, a **private message** is a message sent by a member to another member and will be visible only to them.

For instance, members can send an email to the Administrator from our sample forum after navigating to a post made by a member with the username **admin** and selecting the option titled **Send admin an email**. A pop-up window will be displayed as shown below:

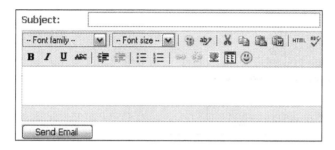

Enter the required information and click on the **Send Email** button to deliver the message as an email. Your email address will be displayed at the top of the dialog box shown above.

> Community Server uses three different types of text editors — **Plain**, **Standard**, and **Enhanced** — for all purposes. You can modify them from the **Site Options** tab from the user profile page. In order to access the user profile page, click on the username link located at the top on the site.

In the same way, you can send a private message to any registered member on the site including Administrator. Clicking on the option titled **Send admin a Private Message** will display a page with the required options to compose a message. Click on the **Post** button to deliver the message to the recipient after entering the requested information.

Let us now examine how to view a private message. For this purpose, click on the link titled **Inbox** from the top right side of the page, as shown below:

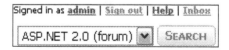

You will see a page as shown in the following screenshot. You can not only read the message but also post replies, which will be delivered to the member who posted the original message. It is also possible to delete a private message if the message is no longer required.

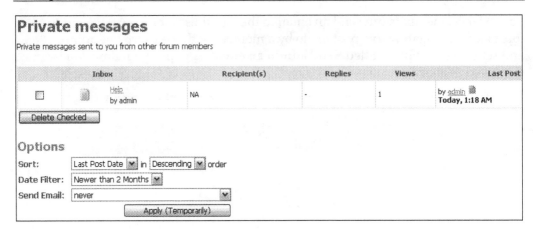

A private message will be displayed in the same manner as a normal thread as shown below:

While an email will be directly delivered to the concerned member, a private message will be posted on the site itself. A member can view the message by navigating to their inbox after logging in to the site.

## Moderating a Post

In order to moderate a post, you should click the button captioned **Moderate**. With the help of this option, a moderator can directly edit or delete the post. A moderator can also split posts, revoke moderation privileges from a user, or merge two different threads having posts with similar subjects. We will discuss more about moderation later in this chapter.

A moderator is a person who is appointed by the Administrator to approve and manage posts.

You will notice an IP address and a few links at the bottom of every post page as shown below:

The first item **127.0.0.1** is the IP address of the member who posted the relevant post. In our sample forum, the Administrator has posted the message from a local installation of Community Server.

 Only Administrators can view the IP addresses of members. For other people the IP address is not shown (but is still stored in the database).

The **Report abuse** link enables a member to report posts that violate community ethics or to report the post as spam to the Administrator. All these reports are stored under **Reporting Forums**, which is created upon installation of Community Server.

The **Quick Reply** link enables a member to post a quick reply instead of a detailed reply. A pop-up window as shown below will be displayed on clicking the link.

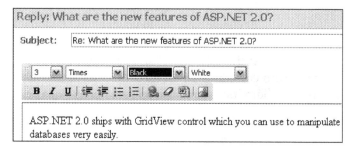

Clicking on the **Post** button will add the message to the thread as shown in the following screenshot:

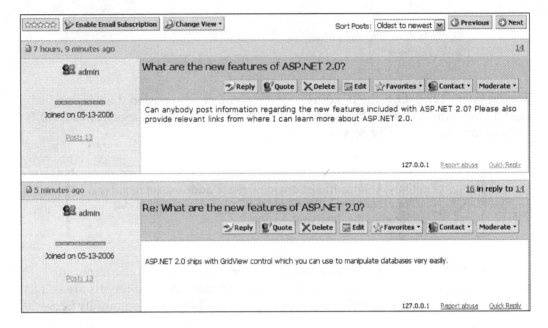

## Sorting and Navigating Posts

You can easily sort the posts using the **Sort Posts** drop-down box located at the top, as shown in the above screenshot. There are two different ways to sort posts: **Oldest to newest** or **Newest to oldest**.

You can also navigate between threads using the **Previous** and **Next** buttons. This feature is useful if the forum contains a lot of threads and requires faster navigation than selecting each one of them individually from the home page of the forums.

# Threads versus Posts

Let us now examine the relationship between threads and posts. If you browse to the home page of the forums, you can see a screenshot as shown on the next page:

| | Forums | Last Post | Threads | Posts |
|---|---|---|---|---|
| | ASP<br>Discuss about Classic ASP. | - | - | - |
| | ASP.NET 1.1<br>Discuss about ASP.NET 1.1 here. | - | - | - |
| | ASP.NET 2.0<br>Discuss about ASP.NET 2.0 here. | Re: What are the new feat...<br>by admin<br>**Today, 2:28 AM** | 1 | 3 |

From the above screenshot, we can infer that there is one thread and three posts under the **ASP.NET 2.0** forum. Hence, there can be several posts under a single thread. Each new submission posted to the forum is considered as a thread.

# Moderating Posts

Normally, threads and posts are published instantly. Sometimes, approval may be required so that you can verify the content of the post before it is published on the forum. Approval has to be given by the person appointed by the Administrator and that person is identified as a **moderator**.

Let us now examine how to moderate a post. Firstly, you should give the required permission for the forum that you would like to moderate. For our sample forum, we will give the permissions for the forum titled **ASP.NET 2.0**. Click on the **Control Panel** link from the top navigation bar and select the link titled **Add new forums, control permissions, etc.** located under the **Forums Administration** section from the **Dashboard**.

Select the **Forums** link available under the drop-down of the **Forums** panel from the left-hand side navigation panel, locate the forum titled **ASP.NET 2.0** on the grid, and select the **Edit** button located on the grid to manage the forum. Alternatively, you can also directly select the forum title captioned **ASP.NET 2.0** to manage it. You will now see a page with the title **Editing Forum: ASP.NET 2.0** with four tabs on it. Click the **Advanced** tab and select the option **Yes** for the setting **Moderate Posts** as shown on the next page and click **Save** button located at the bottom of the page.

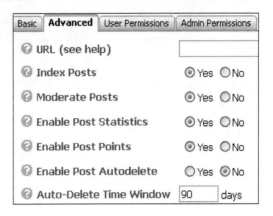

We have successfully given the required permissions to moderate our sample forum named **ASP.NET 2.0**. Hence, from here onwards, whenever a member submits a post it has to be approved by the Administrator before it is visible on the forum.

In order to submit a post that requires approval from a moderator, we should first log out as Administrator and log in as a user. After signing in, select the **Forums** link from the top navigation toolbar, click the forum with the name **ASP.NET 2.0** as shown in the screenshot below:

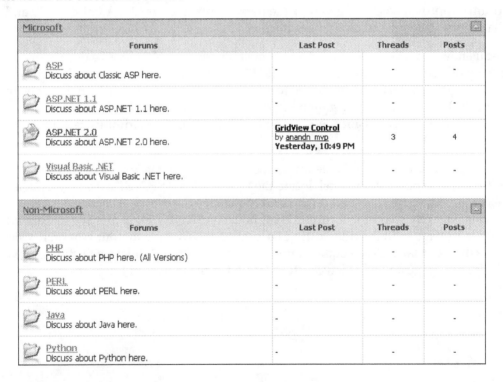

Let us now submit a post by clicking on the **Write a New Post** button. You should enter the required information as discussed earlier. As soon as you click on the **Post** button, a page as shown below will be displayed:

We have now successfully posted a thread that has to be approved by the moderator appointed by the Administrator. For our sample forum, moderator is the Administrator and hence the post will not be visible on the home page of the forums until the Administrator approves it.

You can even browse directly to the relevant sections of the forum by selecting the **(please select)** dropdown as shown in the following screenshot:

As you can see from the above screenshot, you can navigate directly to the **Dashboard**, view private messages, and also navigate to the various forums on the site.

# Approving a Post

In order to approve a post that is awaiting moderation, you should log in as an Administrator. Hence you should sign out and then sign in using the username and password meant for the Administrator.

As soon as you sign in, click on the **Control Panel** link located on the top navigation bar. Select the link titled **Moderate Forums** located under the section **Forums Moderation** as shown below. Alternatively, you can also select the **Forums Moderation** button from the navigation toolbar.

The following page will be displayed on clicking the link **Moderate forums**.

Select the link **Moderate (1)** below the column **Posts to Moderate** to approve the post. You will now view a page as shown below:

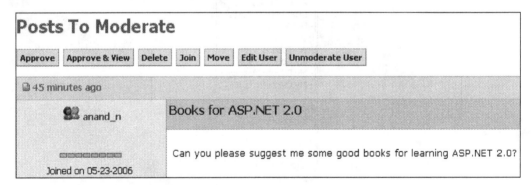

As you will notice, the page contains many buttons on the top row, which can be used for moderating and managing the post.

As soon as you click on the **Approve** button the relevant post will be approved immediately. If there are more posts pending for moderation the resulting page will display those posts. Otherwise, a message **Good news! There is nothing waiting to be moderated** will be displayed. You can check whether the post has been approved or not by clicking the **Moderation Statistics** link from the navigation panel located on the left-hand side.

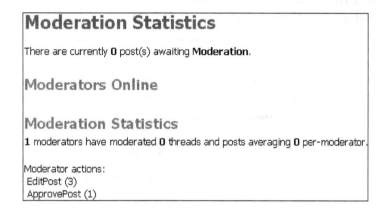

The **Approve and View** button can be used to approve and view the post immediately after the completion of the moderation process. Its function is similar to that of **Approve** button. The only difference is that you can view the post immediately.

The **Delete** button enables you to delete the post without its being approved. This may be required if the post contains material not suitable for the site. Community Server will prompt you to enter the reason for deletion of the post. You can choose one of the options from the **Reason Template** drop-down box as shown in the following screenshot so that you need not type in a reason.

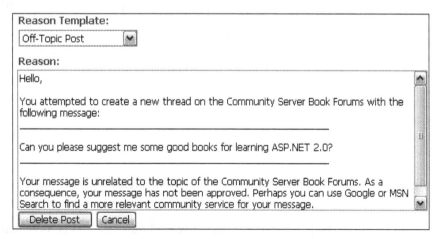

As soon as you click on the **Delete Post** button, the relevant post will be transferred to the **Deleted Posts** forum under the **Administrators** forum group and an email will be sent to the original author of the post.

# Merging Posts

You can merge two different threads using the **Join** button. As soon as you click on it, a pop-up dialog box will be displayed as shown below:

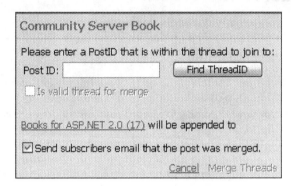

You should enter the **Post ID** that you want to merge with the current active post. We will merge the current post with the one that we posted earlier. In order to locate the **Post ID**, navigate to the previous post by visiting the relevant forum and locate it from the file name of the post. For our sample post, the **Post ID** is **14**. You need to enter this number on the **Post ID** field and click on the **Find ThreadID** button so that Community Server will search for the ID and, if it finds it, will activate the link titled **Merge Threads**

Click on the **Merge Threads** link to merge the current thread with the one we posted previously.

Let us now navigate to the previous post and check whether the posts have been merged or not. Click on the **Exit Control Panel and Return to Site** link, to return to the home page and navigate to the forums home page by selecting the **Forums** link. You will notice that there is only one post that is active. Click on it, scroll down the page, and you can see that our post has been merged with the first post as shown below.

# Moving Posts

Sometimes, members will post threads in wrong forums. For instance, a post meant for discussing **ASP. NET 2.0** related issues might have been posted at the **ASP** forum. In such a situation, as an Administrator, you need to move the thread to the appropriate forum. This can be achieved by using the **Move** functionality provided by Community Server. Let us now examine how to move a post from one forum to another. As a first step, you should post a thread to a wrong forum as shown in the screenshot on the next page:

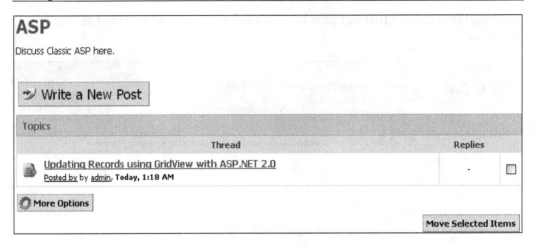

You can also select the **Move Selected Items** button to move post(s).

As you can see from the above screenshot, we have posted a thread meant for the **ASP.NET 2.0** forum into a forum meant for discussing **ASP**. Let us now examine how to move this thread from the **ASP** forum to the **ASP.NET 2.0** forum.

Navigate to the above thread, click on the option titled **Moderate**, and choose the option **Move** as shown below:

As soon as you click on the **Move** option, you will see a page with the caption **Move Thread**. Expand the forum group named **Microsoft** from the **Move To** section and select the required forum to which you wish to move the thread as shown on the next page.

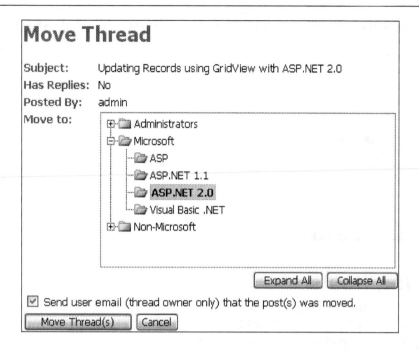

Alternatively, a moderator can also move the post while approving it. Click the **Move** button available on the **Posts To Moderate** page as shown in the screenshot in the *Approving a Post* section.

As you can observe from the above screenshot, we have moved the thread to the correct forum, **ASP.NET 2.0**. Community Server will automatically deliver an email to the member who posted the wrong thread with a message that the thread posted has been moved to the correct forum. Finally, click the button captioned **Move Thread(s)** to move the thread. A message **Oops! There are either no posts or due to a filter there are no posts to display** will be displayed since there are now no active threads on the **ASP** forum.

You will be able to view the moved thread if you browse to the **ASP.NET 2.0** forum.

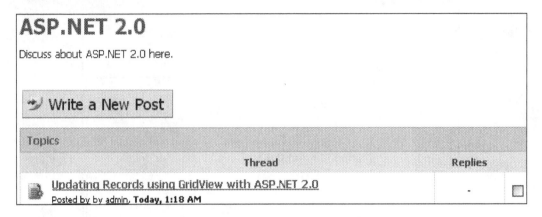

# Locking Posts

As your site matures, some posts on the site become outdated. As an Administrator, you need to either remove or restrict further responses to those posts. Sometimes, you may feel that a particular thread will be useful and other members of the community will benefit from the posted content. In such a situation, you can lock the thread. When a thread is in locked state, members cannot post a reply but can view the content.

You can lock the thread very easily using Community Server. You need to log in as an Administrator and browse to the relevant forum. Click on the **Moderate** drop-down and you will be able to see an option titled **Lock**. As soon as you click on it, the relevant thread will be locked.

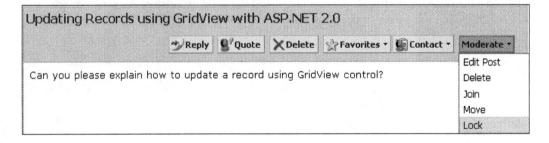

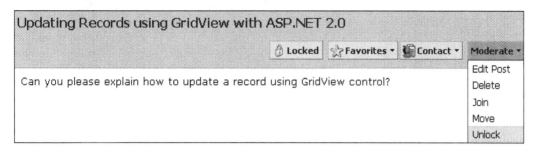

If you feel that the thread needs to be reopened then you can unlock the thread using the **Unlock** option as shown above.

From the above screenshot, you will notice that the **Reply, Quote,** and **Delete** buttons are not visible when a thread is locked.

 As an Administrator, you can edit the profile of a member registered on the site using the **Edit User** option located under the **Moderate** drop-down box.

# Managing Forum Settings Globally

Let us now examine some of the settings that you have to manage while working with forums. By default there is no need to modify the value of these settings but sometimes there will be a requirement to modify some of them.

In order to manage forum settings globally, you need to click on the link titled **Global Forum Settings** from the navigation panel located under the **Forums** section on the left side of the **Control Panel** page. You will see a page with five tabs as shown in the screenshot on the next page.

| General | Editing | Attachments | Duplicates & Flooding | Popular Posts |

## General Post Settings

| | | |
|---|---|---|
| Enable RSS Feeds for public forums | ● Yes | ○ No |
| Enable Thread Status Tracking | ○ Yes | ● No |
| Enable Post Mouse-Over Popup | ○ Yes | ● No |
| Allow User Posting as Anonymous | ○ Yes | ● No |
| Allow Post Tagging | ● Yes | ○ No |
| Default Items/Feed | 25 | |
| Threads/Page | 20 | |
| Post/Page | 15 | |
| Mark New Posts as Read (Days) | 7 | |

As you can see from the above screenshot these settings are related to threads and their management. It is extremely crucial to understand these settings so that you can manage forums very effectively as you gain more experience with the system. You should also note the fact that the changes made to the above settings will affect all active forums on the site. Let us now examine the settings under each tab in detail

# Managing General Post Settings

With the help of the options on the **General** tab, you can manage threads and posts. You can specify how many threads and posts should appear under each forum and other related settings.

**Enable RSS Feeds for public forums**: If this is enabled, forums will generate RSS feeds for all active and public forums.

**Enable Thread Status Tracking**: If this is enabled, the status of threads can be tracked by those users who started the thread. You can specify the status as *Not Set*, *Answered*, or *Not Answered* once the topic under discussion is successfully resolved. By default, this setting is disabled.

**Enable Post Mouse-Over Popup**: If this is enabled, a pop-up text will be displayed when a user holds the mouse pointer over the topic link. By default, this setting is disabled as it sends back all the text of the message and consumes additional bandwidth.

**Allow User Posting as Anonymous**: If this is enabled, all users can contribute to the forums even though they haven't registered on the site. By default, this setting is disabled. That means only registered users can post threads to the forums.

**Allow Post Tagging**: If this is enabled, users can tag their posts with the help of tags. They can later use those tags to browse the posts on the site.

**Default Items/Feed**: This denotes the number of threads that should be displayed on the RSS feed. By default, the value is 25. You can modify it as per your requirement.

**Threads/Page**: This denotes the total number of threads that should be displayed on the relevant page. The default value is 20. If you set this to 5 then each forum page will display 5 single threads and after that it shows the next 5 posts on the second page.

**Post/Page**: This denotes the total number of posts that should be displayed on the relevant thread page. The default value is 15. If you set this to 5 then each thread will display 5 posts submitted by various users and after that it shows the next 5 posts on the second page.

You can submit any number of replies under a single thread.

**Mark New Posts as Read (Days)**: Sometimes, forums displays that there are no posts made during a particular interval. You can specify that interval in days using this setting. For instance, if you specify 15 and there are no posts made on the forums then Community Server shows that there are no post(s) made during the last 15 days when a user browses the forum. The default value is 7.

# Managing Post Editing

With the help of the options on the **Editing** tab, you can manage editing-related activities for the posts made on the site.

**Require Edit Notes**: If this is enabled, users should enter a reason if they edit a particular post after its publication. This is termed **Edit Notes** as per forums parlance.

**Display Edit Notes**: If this is enabled, edit notes will be displayed at the bottom of each message before the user signature.

**Edit Post Body Age Limit (in minutes)**: If this is enabled, a user can edit the title of the post up to certain time limit set here. By default, it is set to 0 minutes. This means that a user can edit the title of the post at any time without any restriction.

# Managing Attachments

With the help of the options on the **Attachment** tab, you can control and manage attachments-related tasks. For instance, you can restrict your users to upload only files with the .ZIP extension. Let us now look at the various settings in detail:

**Enable Attachments**: If this is enabled, users can upload files such as code files when submitting their posts. By default this setting is enabled.

**Allow File Extension Types**: This field specifies the extensions of those files that are allowed to be uploaded while attaching files. By default the extensions populated in **Allow File Extension Types** field are **zip;cab;jpg;gif;png;mpg;mpeg;avi;wmv;wma; mp3;ra;rar;rm;sql;txt**.

**Max File Size (In Kilobytes)**: This field denotes the maximum size of file that can be uploaded as an attachment. The default value is 64 Kilobytes.

**Enable inline image attachments**: If this is enabled, attachments that are images are automatically displayed inline within messages. By default, this setting is disabled.

**Inline Image Attachment Dimensions**: In this field, you can specify the width and height of the image that will be inserted inline. These settings are useful to ensure large images are scaled appropriately.

**Supported Inline Image Types**: This field specifies the extension of those image files that can be inserted inline i.e. within the body of the post. The default extensions are **jpg;gif;bmp;pcx;png;pic**.

# Managing Duplicates and Flooding

With the help of the options on the **Duplicates & Flooding** tab, you can control the posts to enhance the functioning of your forum.

**Allow Duplicate Posts**: If this is enabled, a user can publish the same content as one of the previous postings. This feature is disabled by default as it will create confusion among users.

**Duplicate Post Interval (In Minutes)**: This field denotes the time interval set for publishing a duplicate post. The default value is 15 minutes. For example, if you publish a post now then you cannot submit another post with the same content within 15 minutes of posting the first one.

**Enable Flood Interval Checking**: If this is enabled, members cannot submit posts at immediate intervals. This means that there will be some time limit between the submission of one post and another one. By default, this setting is disabled.

**Minimum time between Posts**: This field denotes the minimum time limit that is required between submission of successive posts. The default value is 15 minutes. For example, if you publish a post now then you cannot submit another post until the expiry of the first 15 minutes from the time of submission of the first post.

# Managing Popular Posts

With the help of the options on the **Popular Posts** tab, you can specify how to display those posts that are popular on your site.

**Popular Post Replies**: This field denotes the total number of posts that are required for a particular thread to become popular. By default, the value is 15 posts. For instance, if you publish a thread now then it will become popular after 15 members reply to that thread.

**Popular Posts Views**: This field denotes the total number of views that are required for a particular thread to become popular. By default, the value is 200 views. For instance, if you publish a thread now then it will become popular only after 200 views or hits.

**Popular Posts Age (In Days)**: This field denotes the number of days a popular post should be active. By default, it is 3 days.

# Working with Ranks

As an Administrator, you can specify ranks for your members. You can set a specific range within which a member can be assigned an appropriate rank. A rank denotes how active a user is within the forum. For instance, a member who posts a minimum of 5 posts can be recognized as a Beginner and those who post more than 50 posts as Advanced. Let us now examine the steps involved in the creation and management of ranks.

# Creating a Rank

Firstly, navigate to the **Dashboard** by selecting the **Control Panel** link after logging in as an Administrator and click the link titled **Administration**. Pull down the **Forums** panel from the navigation bar located on the left-hand side and click **Manage Ranks**. You will see a new page with an empty grid. In order to create a new rank, select the **Add A New Rank** button and enter the required information on the pop-up dialog box as shown in the following screenshot. Click on the **Save** button to add the rank to the forum.

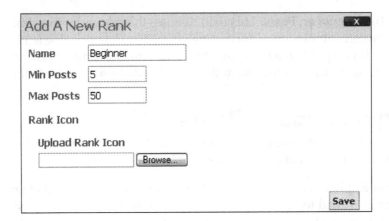

From the above screenshot, you can infer that a member is recognized as a **Beginner**, if that particular member has submitted more than **5** but less than **50** posts. For instance, if a user submits 20 posts then that user is recognized as a Beginner on the forum. You can also upload an icon, preferably an image that can be identified with the rank you created. As soon as you click the **Save** button the rank will be added to the grid as shown below:

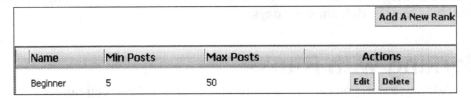

# Viewing the Rank

In order to view the rank which we created, exit from the **Dashboard**, navigate to the home page of the forum and select a post under any forum. If you have posted more than 5 posts then you can view the rank as shown on the next page.

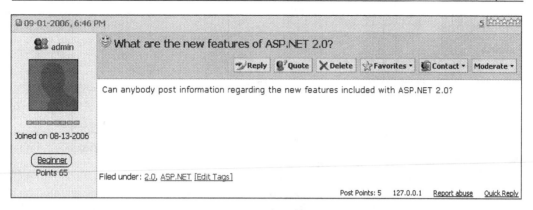

From the above screenshot, you will notice that the user named **admin** is a **Beginner**. In the same way, you can create any number of ranks depending upon your requirements. You can easily manage the created ranks by selecting the **Edit** and **Delete** buttons. Community Server will prompt you to confirm the action when you delete a particular rank.

# Analyzing the Forums Home Page of an Administrator

In the previous sections, you have learned about the creation and management of forums. Let us now examine the elements inside the forums home page of an Administrator as shown on the next page.

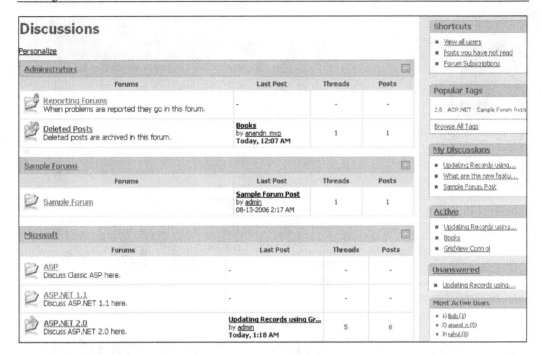

As you can see each forum group has been placed inside a separate panel. Each panel can be expanded and collapsed as per your requirements. For instance, if you click on the group name titled **Microsoft**, a new page will be displayed that will contain only those forums filed under the **Microsoft** group.

 You should note that these features are available for both users and Administrators.

Alternatively, you can also navigate to the relevant forums and posts by selecting the required option from the links located below the top navigation bar inside each forum page as shown below:

Community Server Book » Microsoft » ASP.NET 2.0 » Updating Records using GridView with ASP.NET 2.0

The forum group panels can be expanded and collapsed using the appropriate arrow located on the top right-hand side as you can see on the screenshot in the next page.

| Microsoft | | | | ⊟ |
|---|---|---|---|---|
| **Forums** | **Last Post** | **Threads** | **Posts** |
| ASP<br>Discuss Classic ASP here. | - | - | - |
| ASP.NET 1.1<br>Discuss ASP.NET 1.1 here. | - | - | - |
| ASP.NET 2.0<br>Discuss ASP.NET 2.0 here. | **Updating Records using Gr...**<br>by admin<br>**Today, 1:18 AM** | 5 | 6 |
| Visual Basic .NET<br>Discuss Visual Basic .NET here. | - | - | - |

By default, the arrow located on the top right side in the above screenshot is pointed upwards. If you click on it, the arrow will point downwards and the forums under that group will not be visible as shown below:

Let us now examine the elements located on the right side of the forums home page.

# Shortcuts

The first section, **Shortcuts,** provides the required options for the effective management of members and posts.

## Viewing a List of All Users

You can quickly view a list of all registered members on the site by selecting the link titled **View all users**. Clicking on it will display a page with various options.

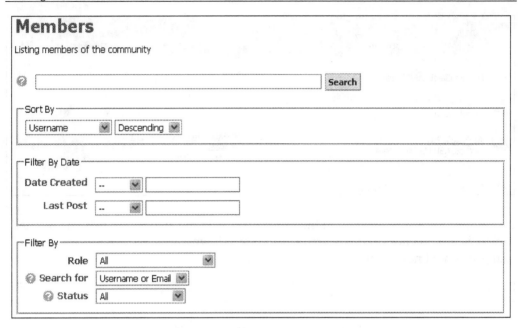

As soon you click on the **Search** button without entering any information, the results will be displayed in a grid as shown below:

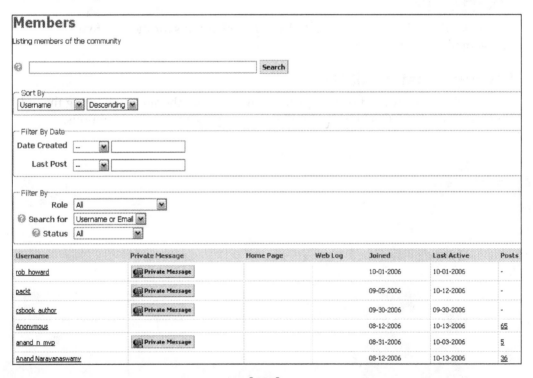

You can initiate the search by entering or picking up any one of the criteria. We will now search for a particular user named **packt** by entering the username and selecting the option **Username** from the **Sort By** panel. The final result will appear as shown below:

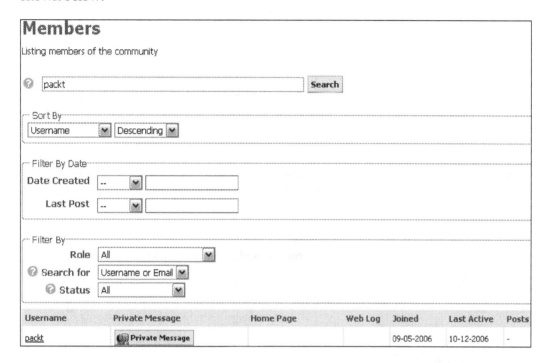

## Posts you have Not Read

This page will display all those posts on the forum that you have not read so far. These can be either new or old posts.

## Forum Subscriptions

With the help of this option, you can subscribe to forums. The benefit of subscriptions is that you will be notified by email if a new thread has been posted on the site.

# Popular Tags

The **Popular Tags** section displays a list of all the tags currently in use on the site. Selecting a tag will enable you to navigate to the relevant post on the forum in which we have filed that tag as shown on the next page.

**Browse by Tags**

All Tags » 2.0

ASP.NET

**What are the new features of ASP.NET 2.0?**

Can anybody post information regarding the new features included with ASP.NET 2.0?

Posted to ASP.NET 2.0 (Forum) by admin on September 1, 2006

If you have filed a particular tag for more than one post then the system will display all of them. You can view a list of all the tags by selecting the link titled **Browse All Tags**.

 As your site grows, you will notice that certain tags are displayed in a bigger font while others are in a smaller font. It is the result of the popularity of the tags and this feature is called "tag cloud".

# My Discussions

The **My Discussions** section displays a list of active posts posted by the logged in user on the forum.

# Active

The **Active** section includes a list of all those posts that are actively discussed on the forum on the date on which the home page has been accessed.

# Unanswered

The **Unanswered** section provides a list of all those posts that are posted on the forum but with no replies.

# Most Active Users

The **Most Active Users** section provides a list of all registered users who are active in posting and replying to threads on the forums.

# Analyzing the Forums Home Page of a User

The home page from the point of view of a user, as shown in the following screenshot, looks very similar to that of the Administrator, which we have seen while discussing the previous section. The only notable difference is that forums under the **Administrators** group are not displayed. As noted previously, it will be visible only to the Administrators.

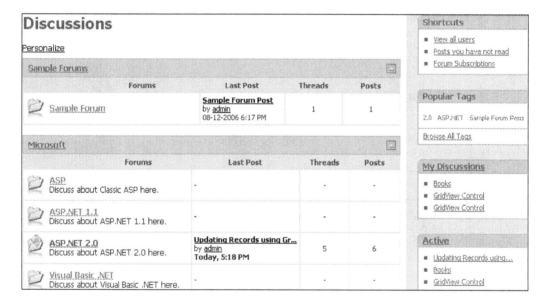

 It is not necessary to log in to the site to view the forums home page.

# Personalizing the Home Page

With the help of the personalization feature, you can quickly filter the list of forums displayed. If you observe the screenshot on the previous page, you can see a link titled **Personalize**. Clicking on it will change the home page as shown below:

Return To Personalized View

| Sample Forums (Displayed: Yes ) | | | | |
|---|---|---|---|---|
| **Forums** | **Last Post** | **Threads** | **Posts** | **Displayed** |
| Sample Forum | **Sample Forum Post** by admin 08-12-2006 6:17 PM | 1 | 1 | Yes |

If you click on the link titled **Yes** located beside the group name **Sample Forums**, the title of the link will be changed to **No** as shown in the following screenshot, indicating that the home page will not display the posts filed under **Sample Forums** group.

Return To Personalized View

| Sample Forums (Displayed: No ) | | | | |
|---|---|---|---|---|
| **Forums** | **Last Post** | **Threads** | **Posts** | **Displayed** |
| Sample Forum | **Sample Forum Post** by admin 08-12-2006 6:17 PM | 1 | 1 | Yes |

If you click on the link titled **Return To Personalized View** now, the home page will not show the forums under the group **Sample Forums** as shown on the next page.

| Personalize | | | | |
|---|---|---|---|---|

**Microsoft**

| | Forums | Last Post | Threads | Posts |
|---|---|---|---|---|
| | ASP<br>Discuss about Classic ASP here. | - | - | - |
| | ASP.NET 1.1<br>Discuss about ASP.NET 1.1 here. | - | - | - |
| | ASP.NET 2.0<br>Discuss about ASP.NET 2.0 here. | **Updating Records using Gr...**<br>by admin<br>**Today, 5:18 PM** | 5 | 6 |
| | Visual Basic .NET<br>Discuss about Visual Basic .NET here. | - | - | - |

**Non-Microsoft**

| | Forums | Last Post | Threads | Posts |
|---|---|---|---|---|
| | PHP<br>Discuss about PHP here. (All Versions) | - | - | - |
| | PERL<br>Discuss about PERL here. | - | - | - |
| | Java<br>Discuss about Java here. | - | - | - |

# Summary

Forums are an effective tool for enabling people to easily discuss and share information. Forums can be deployed either as a knowledge base for providing support to your customers or for discussion among peers. This chapter provided a comprehensive explanation about the creation, management, usage, and personalization of forums capabilities, included within Community Server. We also discussed the elements included within the home page of an Administrator and user.

The next chapter will explain how to create and manage photo and file galleries.

**5**

# Working with Galleries

In this chapter, you will master how to make use of the photo and file gallery capabilities available with Community Server. The chapter is divided in two parts; the first part examines the concepts behind the building of a photo gallery by creating a sample gallery, which uses the logos supplied by Microsoft for its Most Valuable Professionals (MVPs). In the second part of the chapter, we will examine the creation of a file gallery by creating a sample gallery using some sample files. After reading this chapter, you will have gained sufficient expertise to create and maintain photo and file galleries.

## About Galleries

Before the advent of the Internet, people used to keep photos of family, friends, weddings, vacation trips, and so on in a hard-copy album. While albums haven't been completely replaced by online tools, it is cumbersome to maintain and manage those hard-copy albums. Moreover, the albums will become unusable over a period of time. With the advent of technology, people thought about showcasing photos online. Initially, people started to put their photos on their personal websites as separate images. Later on automated online photo galleries provided by third-party websites caught on. Many companies began to develop custom photo gallery applications as well.

With online photo galleries, you can quickly navigate between photos, view thumbnails of photos, add comments to photos, easily share photos with other people, and do much more. There are separate applications available only for the purpose of creating galleries as noted above. But Community Server provides a powerful photo and file gallery tool along with its other core applications, blogs and forums.

Community Server supports a File Transfer Protocol (FTP) gateway that allows people to upload, download, and organize files efficiently, controlled through the Community Server authentication mechanism. Instead of using FTP to download each and every file, you can just browse to the gallery and download the required files as and when they are needed. Moreover, you can organize these files in separate groups. Hence, your users can not only browse your blog but also can view your photo and file galleries.

# Building a Photo Gallery

A photo gallery is a common feature for displaying pictures on personal websites. It provides you with an intuitive way to blend photo management impeccably into a website whether it is a small personal site or a large community site.

# Creating a Photo Gallery: Getting Started

Before proceeding further you should log in as a user with Community Server administration privileges. This can be done by visiting the home page and signing in using the Administrator username and password you configured during installation.

Like blogs and forums, a photo gallery also has a separate home page. It can be viewed by visiting the Community Server home page and clicking the link titled **Photos**. By default, the installer creates a sample photo gallery called **Sample** and you can view a sample photo filed under the gallery on the home page. However, you can create your own galleries and add photos to them. We will examine all the required steps for the creation of a photo gallery with a help of a sample photo gallery in the forthcoming sections. We will use the pictures supplied by Microsoft for those who have won the Most Valuable Professional (MVP) award.

In order to create a photo gallery, click on the **Control Panel** link from the top navigation bar of the home page. You will see a new page with the title **Dashboard**. Click on the link titled **Add new galleries, control permissions, etc.** located under the **Photo Administration** heading to navigate to the **Site Administration** page.

 Alternatively, you can also access the **Site Administration** page by clicking on the **Control Panel** link and then selecting the **Administration** link from the navigation bar located at the top of the page.

You will now see a set of seven links under the **Photos** section as shown in the following screenshot:

Before creating a photo gallery on the site, you should first create photo gallery groups so that you can file each gallery under a specific gallery group. Let us examine how to create a gallery group for our sample photo gallery.

## Creating a Gallery Group

In order to create a gallery group, click on the link titled **Gallery Groups** available in the **Photos** panel. You can see that a group with the name **Sample Photo Galleries** has been automatically created by the installer.

For our sample photo gallery, we will create a group with the name **MVP**. To create this group, click on the **Add New Group** button and enter the required information as shown in the following screenshot:

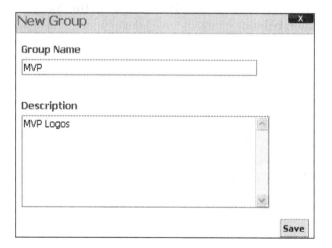

Clicking the **Save** button will add the group named **MVP** to the grid inside the **Groups** page as shown on the next page.

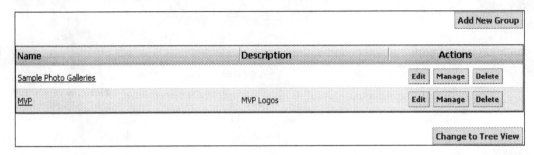

In the same way, you can create another group for your gallery depending upon your requirements.

You can edit the group name and description by selecting the **Edit** button. You can directly manage any group by clicking the **Manage** button from the appropriate row. You can also modify the look and feel of the page to tree-view format, if you prefer, since it will give you more control over the user interface. We have now created the gallery group required for our sample photo gallery. Let us now examine the creation of a gallery.

## Creating a Photo Gallery

In order to create a photo gallery, click on the **Create New Gallery** link located under the **Photos** panel on the left side of the **Site Administration** page. You will see a page with six tabs as shown below:

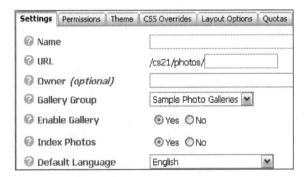

You can also create a gallery by selecting the **Manage** button from the appropriate row on the **Gallery Groups** page. The **Gallery Group** drop-down list will be automatically populated with the relevant gallery groups while creating a new gallery.

Let us discuss these tabs in detail:

## Settings

The various options available when the **Settings** tab is clicked are described below:

**Name**: You can specify the name of the gallery. For our sample photo gallery, we will give the name as **MVP Logos**.

**URL**: You can specify a URL to identify a gallery e.g. **mvp**.

**Owner**: You can also enter a name of the owner who manages the new gallery. This field is to be filled in with the username of a registered member.

**Gallery Group**: You need to select the appropriate gallery group from the **Gallery Group** drop-down box. For our sample gallery, we should select the group named **MVP**, which we created previously.

**Enable Gallery**: By default, the gallery that we created is enabled. If required you can select **No** and then enable it when you are ready to launch the gallery. If disabled, the gallery will not be visible outside the **Dashboard**.

**Index Photos**: By default, the photo galleries are indexed for searching purposes. You should select **No** if you don't want to include your photo gallery to be indexed.

**Default Language**: Finally, select the desired language from the **Default Language** drop-down box.

Since we are entering the URL as **mvp**, our sample photo gallery can be accessed by supplying the URL `http://localhost/cs21/photos/mvp/default.aspx`.

 The URL is also called an **AppKey**.

## Permissions

The **Permissions** tab provides the facility to give access rights to the various kinds of users. While registered users can view and post comments to the photos inside the gallery, Administrators can perform all these tasks by default. You can modify these permissions and also give access to moderators, if you prefer, using the various options.

# Theme

With the help of the **Theme** tab, you can alter the appearance of your photo gallery from a list of available options. As soon as you select a theme, its preview will be displayed on the page as shown below. The page also displays a description of the selected theme.

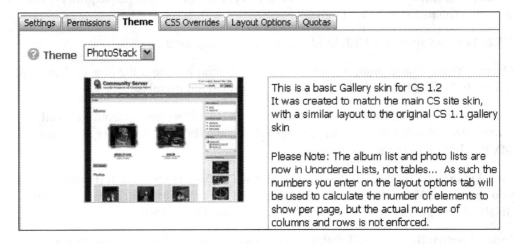

# CSS Overrides

The **CSS Overrides** tab enables you to supply Cascading Style Sheet (CSS) tags for changing the appearance of the themes. We will discuss more about CSS overrides in Chapter 8.

# Layout Options

With the help of **Layout Options** tab, you can modify the way in which the photos should be arranged and displayed on the photo gallery. Let us examine the settings inside the tab in detail.

**Photo Listing Arrangement**: You can specify the total number of columns and rows that should be displayed when viewing a list of photos. By default, it is 4 columns and 4 rows.

**Photos Sort Option**: You can specify how your photos should be sorted when you view the photos inside your gallery. You will view a list of options on clicking the drop-down box as shown on the next page.

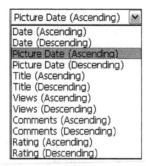

For instance, if you select **Date (Ascending)** then the photos will be sorted according to the ascending order of the date on which the photos were posted into the gallery. The default option is **Picture Date (Ascending)**, which means that photos will be sorted as per the original date of the photos.

## Quotas

The **Quotas** tab lets you specify the photo and disk space limits for the gallery as described below:

**Photo Quota:** This option allows you to specify the maximum number of photos that are allowed inside our photo gallery.

**Disk Quota (kb):** This option allows you to specify the maximum amount of disk space in KB that is allowed for the gallery.

You should note that the changes to these settings affect only the gallery that you are creating and not to the whole site.

Finally, click on the **Save** button to create our new gallery named **MVP Logos**. As soon as the gallery is created, you will be taken to the **Galleries** page where you will see a list of all the galleries created on the site including the default gallery named **Sample**, which is created by the installer.

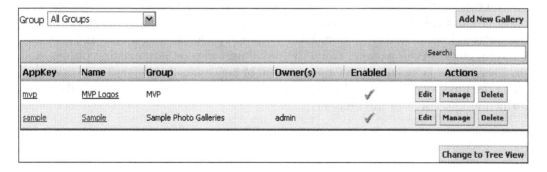

As you can see from the previous screenshot, the grid displays a list of all the galleries created on the site. You can filter galleries according to the relevant gallery group by selecting a group from the **Group** drop-down list at the top of the page. The **AppKey** column denotes the URL of the relevant gallery as we noted earlier.

# Adding Photos

We have successfully created a photo gallery. The next step is to add photos to the gallery. In order to add a new photo to the gallery click the **Manage** button in the relevant row inside the grid on the **Galleries** page. The **Photo Management** page with the title **My Photo Dashboard** will be displayed as shown in the screenshot.

You can also select the **My Photos** link from the Control Panel to manage your photo gallery.

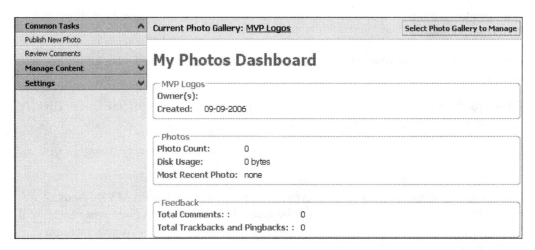

As you can see from the screenshot, the **Dashboard** displays important information regarding our gallery. You can directly navigate to the gallery by clicking the link on the **Current Photo Gallery** section. The navigation panel on the left side is the main building block for our gallery. You will upload new photos, edit existing photos, and review comments including the management of tags and other related information using the links available here. We will examine each one of these options in the forthcoming sections of this chapter.

You can switch photo galleries by clicking the **Select Photo Gallery to Manage** button from the **Photo Management** page.

You can add new photos to the gallery by clicking the **Publish New Photo** link located under the **Common Tasks** section. As soon as you click on the link, the **Publish New Photo** page appears with many options and tabs that are explained as follows:

## Content

Firstly, you need to enter the required information for the options given on the **Content** tab. The options on the other tabs are, however, optional but you need to understand them in order to work with the system as your site grows. Let us examine each one of the options in detail:

**Photo To Upload**: You need to specify the photo that has to be uploaded in this field. You can locate the required photo using the **Upload Photo** button. Clicking on it will display a pop-up dialog box as shown in the following screenshot:

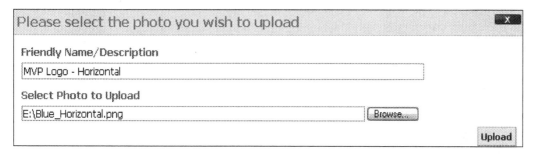

You can provide a small description of the photo in the **Friendly Name/Description** field and choose a photo in the **Select Photo to Upload** field by clicking the **Browse** button. As soon as you click the **Upload** button, the above displayed name and the path will be automatically populated inside the relevant fields of the **Publish New Photo** page. You will also notice that the **Photo To Upload** field will be modified to **File** and a **Remove** button is also visible to remove the uploaded file.

**Subject**: As noted above, this field will display what we have entered in the **Friendly Name/Description** field on the above pop-up dialog box. You can, however, modify it if you wish to do so.

**Tags**: As discussed in previous chapters, tags enable you to organize your gallery very effectively. The relevant photo in the gallery will be automatically displayed as soon as you click on a tag from the gallery page. For our sample gallery, we will enter **MVP, Microsoft** as tags. You can enter any number of tags but they should be separated by semicolons or commas.

 Once you have added the required tags, you can click the **Select Tags** button to choose one of them while adding another photo to the gallery.

**Description**: You can enter a short summary that conveys the meaning of the photo that you are going to upload. For our sample photo gallery, we have entered the description as **This is the official logo supplied by Microsoft for the MVPs.**

The **Publish New Photo** page will appear as shown in the screenshot below, after entering all the required information as explained above.

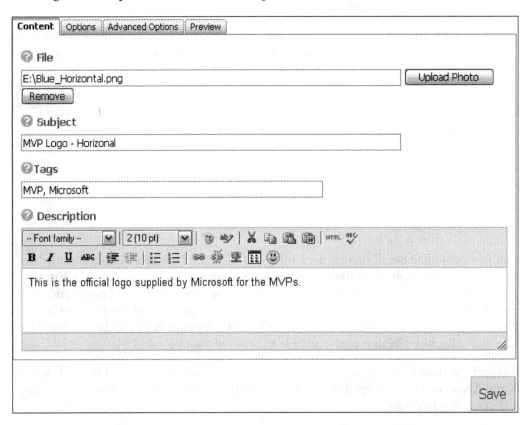

We have now entered all the required information for adding a photo to the gallery. However, you need to understand the settings included in other tabs that you can see from the above screenshot. Let us now examine them in detail:

# Options

With the help of the **Options** tab, you can enter additional information about your photo as explained below:

**Name**: You can enter a name for the photo. This name will be used on the link instead of the PostID.

**Excerpt**: You can specify a short description or a brief note about the photo on this field.

**Post Date**: You can specify the date and time when you would like the photo to be published on the site. To enter month you just need to select the default month available in the field and key in the first alphabet of the month you want to enter in the field. The relevant month will be automatically displayed. Thus if you want to enter **June** then type **J** after selecting the default month this will display **January**. Then press **J** once again that will display **June** in the field.

# Advanced Options

The **Advanced Options** tab enables you to specify advanced settings relating to the photo such as comments, ratings, and other related information. The tab contains several options and they are explained below:

**Is this Photo Published**: If this is enabled, the photo will be immediately published and visible for others. If this is disabled, the photo will not be visible outside the **Dashboard**.

**Enable Comments to your blog**: If this is enabled, readers can post comments to the photo in the gallery.

**Comment Moderation**: This option allows you to specify that the comments need to be approved by the Administrator before being displayed.

**Email Feedback Notifications**: This option allows you to specify what type of feedback the owner of the gallery will receive.

**Enable Ratings**: If this is enabled, members can rate the photo in the gallery.

**Enable Trackbacks**: If this is enabled, trackbacks will be made on all outgoing links of the gallery. The default setting will be determined by your global gallery setting.

**Enable Order Prints**: If this is enabled, the member/owner has the option to send photos to Shutterfly, which is an online service that prints and delivers digital photos.

## Preview

The **Preview** tab provides a facility to view the photo as if it appears inside the gallery. The advantage of this feature is that you can immediately modify the photo or settings if you are not satisfied with the preview.

By default, you need not modify any settings except the specification of the required details on the **Content** tab. But if you feel that you require a restricted gallery you can tweak the gallery using the above mentioned settings.

After a final check of the above settings, click the **Save** button to add the photo to the gallery. As soon as you click the button, the photo will be added inside the grid on the **All Photos** page as shown below:

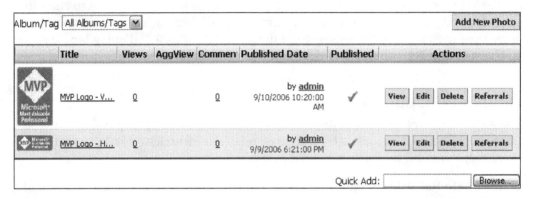

You can add more photos to the gallery by clicking the **Add New Photo** button. For our sample photo gallery, we have added one more photo to the gallery as you can see from the above screenshot.

By default, all the photos that are uploaded to the gallery will be displayed on the grid. However, you can search for a specific photo by selecting a tag from the **Album/Tag** drop-down list. You can quickly add a new photo by clicking the **Browse** button located at the bottom of the page. As soon as you select a photo, the page will be refreshed and the photo will be displayed on the grid, and also in the gallery. You can then modify the uploaded photo by selecting the **Edit** button. The photo will be displayed on the top right-hand side of the **Editing Photo** page.

## Viewing Photos

You can immediately view the uploaded photo by clicking the **View** button. A new page with the photo and other related information as shown on the next page will be displayed.

As you can see, the page shows the subject (at the top) and the description (below the photo). This information was entered by us while adding the photo.

You will also notice an icon with a link titled **View Sizes** below the photo. With the help of this option, you can view the photo in different formats as shown below. This feature is useful if you are dealing with very large photos.

As a user, you can view the photo gallery by clicking the **Photos** link located at the top of the site. The page displays all the photos that we have uploaded to the gallery including the default photo. The first photo will be the one that we have uploaded most recently.

## Navigating Photos

You can easily browse all photos one by one by using the user-friendly navigation links located above the photo.

From the screenshot, you will notice that we are on the second page of the gallery. You can make use of the **Previous** and **Next** links and also the available numbered links.

You can see a detailed statistics, as shown in the following screenshot, about the photo which you are currently viewing on the left side of the gallery page. You can also see a list of tags available. As noted earlier, if you select a tag you will view the photos filed under that tag. You can also manage the gallery using the relevant links inside the **Common Tasks** section, if you have permissions to manage the gallery.

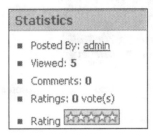

# Posting Comments

Your users can post comments about each of the photos inside the gallery depending upon the settings that you gave while adding the photos. These comments will be either published immediately or after the approval by the Administrator or moderator. As an Administrator, you can manage comments from the **Photo Management** page.

In order to manage comments, we should first post a comment about one of the photos in the gallery. For the purpose of our discussion, we will log in as a user in order to post the comment.

Click the **Photos** link from the top navigation bar and select a photo. A new page with the selected photo at an enlarged size will be displayed. Locate the **Comments** section by scrolling down and enter the required information. For the purpose of our discussion, we have entered a comment—**This photo looks great and cool**.

The comment will be published as soon as you click the **Submit** button and will be visible in the gallery page of that photo as shown below:

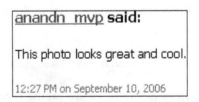

The comment will not be visible if the Administrator has chosen to moderate it. We have not chosen to moderate comments for our sample blog and hence the comment will be displayed in the gallery page immediately. You can visit the website of the user who posted the comment if you click the username after the comment has been posted.

## Managing Comments

As for blogs, you as an Administrator can also manage comments that are posted in the gallery using the **Review Comments** link located under the **Common Tasks** section from the navigation panel on the left side of the **My Photos Dashboard** page. Alternatively, you can also select the **All Comments** link from the **Manage Content** section.

As an Administrator, you can edit comments by selecting the **Edit** button in the **Review Comments** page as shown in the previous screenshot. A comment editor pop-up box will be displayed where you can update the comment. After entering the required information, click the **Publish** button to save the edited comment and return to the **Review Comments** page. You can also directly view or delete the comment using the appropriate buttons.

## Moderating Comments

In order to moderate a comment, you should first upload a photo and enable the comment moderation feature. To enable this functionality, you should choose the option **All comments require approval** from the **Comment Moderation** drop-down list in the **Advanced Options** tab while adding a new photo to the gallery.

You should also make sure to choose the option **All comments require approval** from the **Comment Publishing** drop-down list from the **Default Post Settings** section located under **Settings** panel inside the **Photo Management** page.

For the purpose of our discussion, we will upload a photo to our sample photo gallery and enable comment moderation. After adding the photo to the gallery, navigate to the home page of the gallery, click the photo, and post a comment.

You can directly navigate to the home page of the photo gallery by clicking the link on the **Current Photo Gallery** section at the top of the page.

You will notice that the comment will not appear immediately after clicking the **Submit** button. The next step is to approve the comment by navigating to the **Review Comments** page and selecting the comment, which is pending for approval. Select the **Actions** drop-down list located at the bottom of the page, choose the option **Approve Selected Items** and click the **Go** button to approve the comment as shown below:

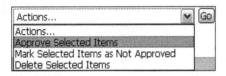

As soon as you select the button, the comment will be approved and it will be visible on the gallery page.

## Managing Tags

As noted above, you can search the photo gallery using tags. You can either create tags separately or can enter the required tags at the time of adding photos to the gallery. Once a tag has been added inside Community Server then you can make use of it in all the photos that you upload to the gallery. In order to manage the tags, click the **Tags / Keywords** link from the **Manage Content** section. You will see a page with a list of all the tags available in the gallery as shown below:

| | | | | | Create New Album/Tag |
|---|---|---|---|---|---|
| **Name** | **Description** | **Last Post** | **Photos** | **Published** | **Actions** |
| aspnetpro | | Sep 10 2006, 03:27 PM | 1 | ✓ | Edit  Delete |
| magazine | | Sep 10 2006, 03:27 PM | 1 | ✓ | Edit  Delete |
| Microsoft | | Sep 10 2006, 10:20 AM | 2 | ✓ | Edit  Delete |
| MVP | | Sep 10 2006, 10:20 AM | 2 | ✓ | Edit  Delete |

From the previous screenshot, you can see the number of photos that are filed under a particular tag. You can also modify or delete a tag by using the relevant buttons. As an Administrator, you can create a new tag by selecting the **Create New Album/Tag** button located at the top of the page. A pop-up dialog box will be displayed where you are required to enter the name and description for the tag. You should select the **Enable Album/Tag** checkbox to enable the tag. Otherwise, the tag will not be visible outside the **Dashboard**.

Let us now create a tag with the name **MSDN** and description **Microsoft Developer Network** for our sample gallery. The **Tags / Keywords** page after saving the tag will appear as shown in a following screenshot:

| Name | Description | Last Post | Photos | Published | Actions |
|------|-------------|-----------|--------|-----------|---------|
| aspnetpro | | Sep 10 2006, 03:27 PM | 1 | ✓ | Edit  Delete |
| magazine | | Sep 10 2006, 03:27 PM | 1 | ✓ | Edit  Delete |
| Microsoft | | Sep 10 2006, 10:20 AM | 2 | ✓ | Edit  Delete |
| MSDN | Microsoft Developer Network | | 0 | ✓ | Edit  Delete |
| MVP | | Sep 10 2006, 10:20 AM | 2 | ✓ | Edit  Delete |

As you can see from the screenshot, the tag **MSDN** appears along with its description. We have entered the other tags while adding photos to the gallery. You can give a description for these tags by selecting the **Edit** button located on each row.

# Working with Albums

There are two methods by which you can categorize your photo gallery. One method is to make use of tags as discussed above. Tags are a new feature introduced in the version 2.1 of Community Server. Prior to the current version, photos were arranged and displayed in the gallery using **Albums**. Albums still exist in version 2.1 but you should enable them from the **Photo Management** page.

In order to enable albums, navigate to the **Photo Management** page inside your gallery and pull down the **Settings** section. Select the **Post Categorization Settings** link and choose **Albums** from the **Categorize Photos Using** drop-down list. As soon as you click the **Save** button, a new link titled **Manage Albums** will be added inside the **Manage Content** section. Moreover, the required options for creating an album will be visible inside the **New Album / Tag** pop-up dialog box that will be explained in the following section.

Community Server automatically converts all the existing tags into albums.

## Creating Albums

In order to create a new album, you should first open the **Tags / Keywords** page by selecting the **Tags / Keywords** link under the **Manage Content** section. Now select the **Create New Album/Tag** button and enter the required information as shown in the screenshot below:

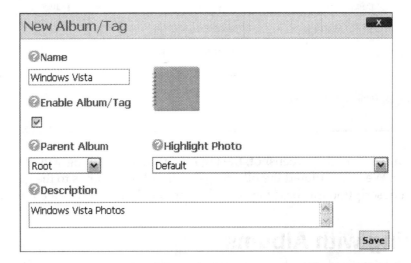

You can nest the above album under any of the available albums by selecting an appropriate option from the **Parent Album** drop-down list. You can use a photo in the gallery to enrich the album. We will retain the settings that are set by default for the purpose of our sample album.

The album **Windows Vista** will be added inside the grid as soon as you click the **Save** button. You can alter the appearance of existing albums by selecting the **Edit** button from the grid.

If you examine the home page of the gallery, you can see some changes to the left side such as activation of album links and the addition of a new section titled **Album List** as shown in the screenshot on next page.

From the above screenshot, you can infer that there are two photos inside the albums named **Microsoft** and **MVP**. You should note that you cannot search the gallery using tags, unless you modify the setting inside the **Post Categorization Settings** page as explained before.

# Managing Albums

In order to manage albums, click the link titled **Manage Albums** located under the **Manage Content** panel on the left-hand side. The **Album Manager** will be displayed in a tree-view format as shown in the screenshot overleaf:

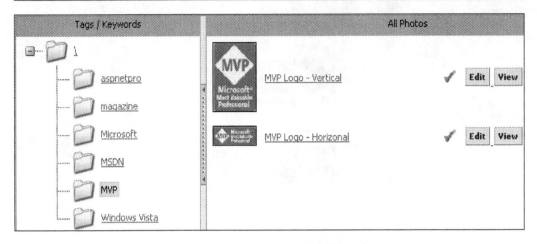

You need to click an album name from the **Tags / Keywords** panel to view the photos inside a specific album. For instance, we have selected an album named **MVP** and the above screenshot displays the photos under it. You can directly modify the content and settings of each one of the photos inside a specific album using the **Edit** button.

You can perform various activities from the **Tags / Keywords** panel. You can not only modify and view the photos inside the specific album but also create or rename an album, and drag-and-drop photos to the album. For instance, to rename an album you just need to click the specific album name from the **Tags / Keywords** panel as shown below:

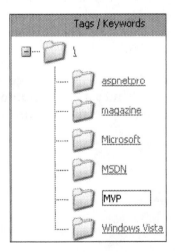

After entering a new name, click anywhere on the page or press *Enter* to save it. You can drag-and-drop a photo from one album to another from the **Album Manager** page. Let us now create another album and examine the drag-and-drop functionality. For this purpose, we will create a new album with the name **ANAND_MVP**.

In order to create a new album from within the **Album Manager** page, right-click the \ (root) folder and select the **Add New** option from the pop-up menu. The page will be refreshed and a new album titled **New Album** will be added inside the **Tags / Keywords** panel. For our sample gallery, we will alter its name and the page will appear as shown below:

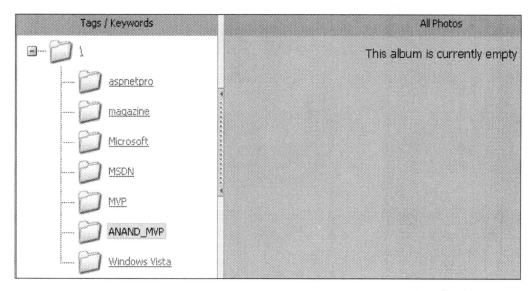

We have now created a new album named **ANAND_MVP**. We will drag a photo from our album **MVP** to the newly created album instead of uploading it. For this purpose, select the album **MVP** and drag a photo from it and drop it on **ANAND_MVP**. You need to hold down the mouse button until the photo has been dropped on the target album.

The page will be refreshed after the completion of the process and the dragged photo will appear inside our new album as shown in the screenshot.

We have now added a photo from one album to another in a very simple way. In a similar way, you can drag-and-drop any number of photos to the required albums using the intuitive interface from the **Album Manager** page.

# Customizing your Photo Gallery

In the previous sections, you learned how to create and manage a photo gallery. Let us now examine how to modify some of the general settings associated with your gallery. In order to modify the settings, expand the **Settings** section from the navigation panel located on the left side of the **Photo Management** page. You will now see a list of options as shown below:

With the help of these options, you can modify the look and feel of your gallery in addition to managing other advanced settings. Let us now examine the usage of each of these settings in detail.

## Modifying the Title and Description

You can modify the title and description of your photo gallery by selecting the **Title and Description** link. You can also enter the required description on the relevant field. By default, the title will be displayed as **MVP Logos**, which was entered while creating the gallery. It is also displayed on the top heading along with the caption **Current Photo Gallery** on the homepage of the gallery page.

You can also supply the required description and keywords for search engines.

## Modifying the Appearance of your Gallery

In order to modify the look and feel of the gallery, you should click the link titled **Change How My Gallery Looks**. It consists of tabs that are explained next:

## Skins

Under the **Skins** tab, you can change the **Theme** of the gallery as shown below:

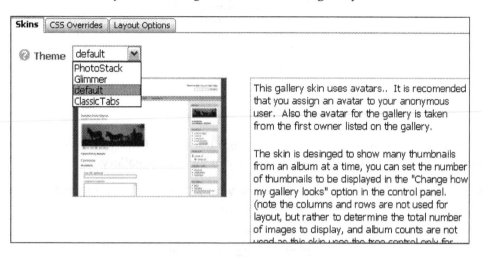

As you can see from the above screenshot, the default theme is named **default**. As soon as you select the theme from the **Theme** drop-down box, a small preview of the selected theme will be displayed on the page along with a short description about it.

## Layout Options

You can also specify various size options for your album and gallery using the **Layout Options** tab. Let us examine the settings inside this tab in detail:

**Album Listing Arrangement**: You can specify the total number of columns and rows that should be displayed when viewing a list of albums. By default, it is 2 columns and 3 rows.

**Photo Listing Arrangement**: You can specify the total number of columns and rows that should be displayed when viewing a list of photos. By default, it is 4 columns and 4 rows.

**Photos Sort Option**: You can specify one of the options seen overleaf to sort the photos inside your gallery.

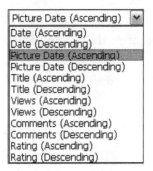

You need to select any one of the options from the above drop-down box and the photos will be displayed accordingly when you view your gallery.

**Albums Sort Option**: You can specify how your albums should be sorted when you view the albums inside your gallery as shown below:

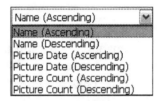

# Configuring the About Page

You can specify the required information that should be displayed when your visitors click on the **About** link present on the home page of your gallery, by clicking the **About My Gallery** link available under the **Settings** section. The **About My Gallery** page appears as shown in the screenshot.

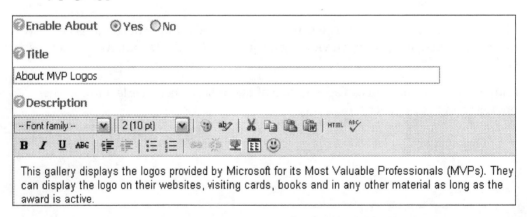

You should note that the **About** link will be visible only if you enable it by using the **Enable About** option. By default, the link is enabled. You can, however, disable it if you don't want to provide the **About** page. The **Title** field will be populated with the relevant title corresponding to your gallery. We have entered a short description for the purpose of our discussion.

The above-mentioned details will be visible when a user clicks the link titled **About** from the home page of the gallery.

# Changing the Categorization Method

You can modify the manner in which the gallery should be displayed by selecting the required option from the **Categorize Photos Using** drop-down list. By default, the photos will be arranged and displayed in the gallery according to tags. You can change it to albums, if you prefer.

 Refer to sections *Managing Tags* and *Managing Albums* for more information regarding the usage of tags and albums.

# Managing Post Settings

You can manage the settings relevant to your gallery by using the **Default Post Settings** and **Advanced Post Settings** options.

## Default Post Settings

You can modify some of the general settings related to the day-to-day management of your gallery by selecting the **Default Post Settings** link. You should note that any modification to any of these settings will be applicable only to new posts. Hence, they are called post-level settings. Let us examine each one of these settings in detail:

**Enable Comments**: If enabled, users can post comments about the photos available in the gallery.

**Comment Publishing**: You can specify the manner in which the comments should be published on the site. By default, all comments will be published immediately in the gallery. As an Administrator, you can select the option to approve comments before they are published to avoid unwanted comments appearing on the site.

**Email Feedback Notifications**: You can specify which notification of feedback you would like to receive through email. You can select **All Feedback** or **All Comments**

from the drop-down list. For instance, if you select **All Comments** then you will receive an email as and when a new comment has been posted on the site.

**Enable Ratings**: If this is enabled, registered users can rate photos in the gallery. A user should be logged into the site in order to rate a photo in the gallery.

**Enable Trackbacks**: If this is enabled, trackbacks will be made on all outgoing links.

**Enable Order Prints:** If this is enabled, photos will be delivered to Shutterfly for printing. The relevant links will be automatically created for this purpose.

**Publish to my aggregate list**: If this is enabled, the photos will be included in the home page of your photo gallery and main syndication feed.

**Publish to site's aggregate list**: If this is enabled, the photos will be included in the RSS feed on the whole site.

**Syndicate Excerpt:** If this is enabled all the excerpts posted while adding a photo to the gallery will be included in the RSS feed instead of the description.

## Managing Advanced Post Settings

With the help of the **Advanced Post Settings** page, you can modify settings related to comments, ratings, and other related options. You should note that any modifications to these settings will affect the whole gallery. Let us examine each one of these settings in detail:

**Allow Replies/Comments**: If this is enabled, replies and comments can be posted to each photo in the gallery. This setting will override any photo-level setting made before.

**Comment Moderation**: The functioning of this setting is similar to that of the **Comment Publishing** setting, which we examined in the previous section. The only difference is that any modification to this setting will override the photo-level setting made in the **Default Post Settings** page.

**Enable Ratings, Enable Trackbacks, Enable Order Prints**: The functioning of these settings is similar to that of the corresponding settings that we examined in the previous section. The only difference is that any modification to these settings on the page will override the photo-level setting set in the **Default Post Settings** page.

**Comment Day Limits**: With the help of this setting, you can specify the number of days for which a new photo in the gallery should accept comments.

For instance, if you set the value to **90 Days** then your visitors can submit comments about the photos inside the gallery for a period of 90 days from the date of their publication. By default, comments can be posted without any limits as the value is set to **Always** as shown in the above screenshot.

## Managing Advanced Photo Settings

You can manage some of the advanced functionalities such as width and height, watermark, and other related settings by selecting the **Advanced Photo Settings** link. As soon as you click the link, a new page with four tabs will be displayed as shown below:

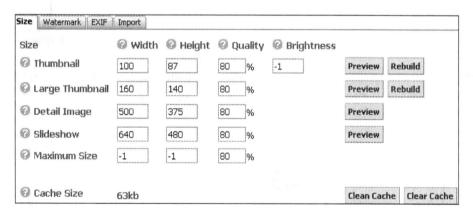

As you can see from the above screenshot, the **Size** tab includes lot of options such as **Width, Height, Quality,** and **Brightness** for managing the sizes of a photo. Community Server will use the values supplied here to display the photos, when you select the options for each photo. You can also view a snapshot of each size by clicking the **Preview** button.

From the previous screenshot, you will see that the size of the cache has been quoted in **kb** (Kilobytes). This means that as you view each photo, some disk space will be consumed by the cache. As your site grows, you will be required to recycle the cache space. This can be done by using the relevant buttons available on the page.

While the **Clean Cache** button enables you to clear all the larger items from the cache space while keeping the thumbnails intact, **Clear Cache** button enables you to completely remove all the items from the cache.

# Watermarking Photos

Watermarking is a mechanism by which you can insert text or images into the photos in the gallery. With Community Server, you can easily insert watermarks. Selecting the **Watermark** tab displays a set of options as shown below:

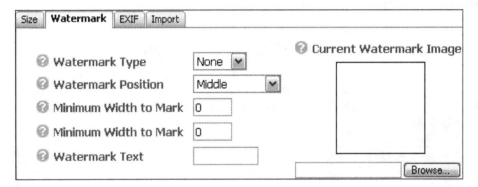

First, you need to specify the type and position of watermark and then the text that should be displayed as a watermark. You can also upload an image that will be displayed as a watermark.

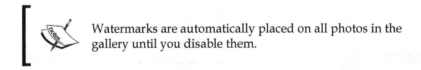

Watermarks are automatically placed on all photos in the gallery until you disable them.

Let us now examine how to insert the text **MVP** on the **Top Left** corner of the photos in the gallery. We need to select the type and position of the watermark from the appropriate drop-down list, enter the required text in the **Watermark Text** field as shown on the next page, and submit the form by clicking the **Save** button located at the bottom of the page.

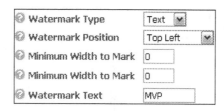

In order to view the watermark, like the one that appears below, you will have to navigate to the home page of your photo gallery and select a photo from it.

You can directly access the home page of a photo gallery by clicking on the link associated with the caption **Current Photo Gallery** from the **Photo Management** page.

# Displaying the Properties of a Photo

You can permit users to view the properties of each and every photo on the **Photo Details** page when they browse the gallery. This will be possible only if you have enabled the EXIF option from the **EXIF** tab on the **Advanced Photo Settings** page. As you will see, EXIF will be enabled by default.

EXIF is a standard for storing metadata with digital pictures and it stands for **Exchangeable Image File Format**. You will find more information at: http://www.exif.org/

You need to select one or more properties from the **EXIF Properties** drop-down list as shown overleaf:

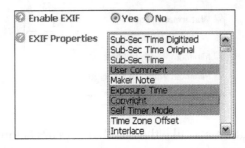

The values of the selected properties will be displayed only if the relevant photo supports them.

# Importing Photos

With the help of this feature, the photos that you have placed manually inside the relevant photo gallery directory located inside the /cs21/photos/ directory can be imported into to your gallery. You can import these photos either to the root of the gallery or to any one of the albums that you have created previously. The required functionality for this feature can be accessed from the **Import** tab located on the **Advanced Photo Settings** page.

For our sample gallery, we will place the photos inside the mvp directory located inside Inetpub\wwwroot\cs21\photos directory. You should note that the **mvp** directory will be automatically created upon the successful creation of a new gallery. As soon as we place the photo inside this directory, the relevant entry on the **Advanced Photo Settings** page will display the number of photos that are located under the relevant gallery directory as shown below:

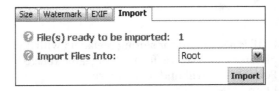

You can import the photo to any one of the albums that you created. For our sample photo gallery, we will import the photo to the album named **MVP**. Select the appropriate album name from **Import Files Into** drop-down box. Clicking the **Import** button will add the photo to the gallery and the following message will be displayed on the bottom of the page.

**1 photo(s) queued for importing. Depending on the number of photos, it may take a while for them to be imported, as only a few are processed at a time.**

Finally, select the **Save** button to finish the process. The imported photo will be displayed depending upon the number of photos in the queue. For our sample photo gallery, we have imported only one photo and hence it should have been properly imported into the appropriate album. The photo can be viewed by navigating to the home page of the gallery.

# Advanced Syndication Settings

With the help of Advanced Syndication Settings, you can enable RSS syndication for your gallery and also for the comments. By default, RSS Syndication for the gallery is enabled. You can, however, enable RSS syndication for comments so that all the comments posted in the gallery will be visible on the RSS feeds.

# Building a File Gallery

In the first part of the chapter, you learned how to create and manage a photo gallery. Community Server additionally supports a web-based file manager. You can use it to post product documentation, code snippets, white papers, and much more. In this section, we will examine how to create and manage a file gallery. We will make use of a sample chapter of one of the books published by **Packt Publishing**, a PowerPoint presentation, and a Word document to illustrate the concepts.

# Getting Started

Firstly, make sure that you are logged in as an Administrator for creating a file gallery. Next, navigate to the **Dashboard** by clicking on the **Control Panel** link from the top navigation bar. Scroll down the page and select the entry titled **Add new folders, control permissions, etc.** located under the section titled **File Administration**. The **Files** section will be displayed with a set of four options on the left side navigation panel as shown below:

The first step is to create a new folder group. A folder group is an organizational tool for file galleries. Next we'll create a folder under the group we created. You cannot upload and manage files without creating a folder and you cannot create a folder without creating a folder group. However, Community Server installer automatically creates a folder group with the name **Sample Downloads**. Hence if you attempt to create a new folder without creating a folder group, the new folder will be created under the **Sample Downloads** group.

## Creating a Folder Group

As explained above, we will create a sample file gallery which will contain the PDF file of a chapter from one of the books published by **Packt Publishing**.

In order to create a folder group, click **Folder Groups** from the **Files** section and select the **Add New Folder Group** button. As soon as you click the button, a pop-up dialog box with the title **New Folder Group** will be displayed. Enter the required name for the folder group and give a short description for it. For our sample file gallery, we have entered the information as shown below:

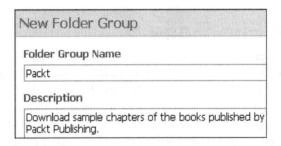

After entering the required information, click the **Save** button located at the bottom of the dialog-box to create a folder group named **Packt**. The group will be added to the grid on the **Folder Groups** page as shown below:

As you can see, Community Server installer automatically creates a folder group with the name **Sample Downloads**.

You can edit or delete a group by selecting the appropriate button from the **Actions** column of the relevant folder group. We have now successfully created a folder group for our sample file gallery. The next step is to create a new folder and then a file in that folder under the above-created group.

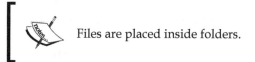 Files are placed inside folders.

# Creating a Folder

In order to create a new folder, select the link titled **New Folder** from the **Files** navigation panel on the left side of the **Site Administration** page.

## Settings

Firstly, you should enter the required information for the various options under the **Settings** tab. For our sample file gallery, we have entered the information as shown below:

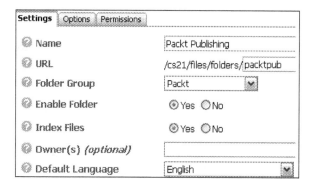

As you can see from the above screenshot, we have selected the folder group that we created in the previous section. The Uniform Resource Locator (URL) for navigating to our sample file gallery will be `http://localhost/cs21/files/folders/packtpub`, where **packtpub** is the value that we gave in the URL field.

By default, all folders are enabled. If required you can disable a folder but it will not be visible outside the **Dashboard**. The file search or index feature is enabled by default. Your users can locate the file while performing a search operation on the file gallery. You can also optionally specify a list of users who wish to access the above folder in the **Owner(s)** field.

## Options

The **Options** tab contains the required settings for the management of files and they are explained overleaf:

**Enable External Links**: If this is enabled, users can download files through redirected URLs. This is a benefit if the files reside in another location and the addition to the file gallery is done to help people find these files. This helps to search the files present in some external location and add them to the file gallery.

**Enable Download Disclaimer**: If this is enabled, a disclaimer will be displayed while downloading files from the gallery. People attempting to download the file will first have to agree with terms displayed in the disclaimer before continuing on to the file download.

**Allowed File Extensions**: You can specify a list of extensions separated by commas. If this is enabled only the files with these extensions with be allowed to be uploaded in the folder.

**Restricted File Extensions**: You can specify a list of extensions separated by commas. The uploading of files with these extensions will be blocked.

## Permissions

The **Permissions** tab provides more options to control the download and upload of files by different users. After checking appropriate permissions, click the **Save** button located at the bottom of the page to create the required folder. The folder will be immediately created and will be visible in the grid on the page as shown below:

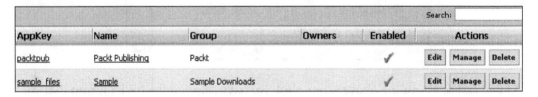

In addition to our sample folder, you can also see a folder named **Sample** that has been automatically created by the installer.

The **Global Permissions** option on the **Files** navigation panel enables you to specify permissions globally to all the folders.

# Managing a Folder

You can modify the settings of folders by selecting the **Manage** button from the appropriate row of the folder on the grid. You can also view and manage folders in the tree-view format by clicking the button captioned **Change to Tree View** at the bottom of the grid.

# Uploading a File

In the previous section, you learned about the creation of a folder group and a new folder under that group. Let us now examine the procedure for uploading files to our sample folder named **Packtpub**.

Click the **Control Panel** link and then select the **My Files** link from the navigation bar located at the top of the page. The **My Files Dashboard** page will be displayed as shown below:

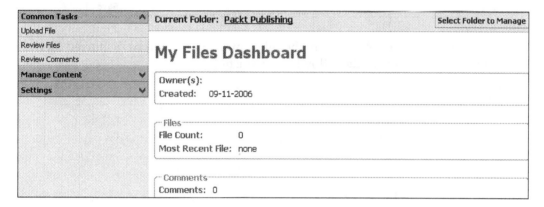

As you can see, the page displays the number of files that have been uploaded to the gallery and also information about comments in addition to the owner information and creation date. The navigation panel on the left-hand side displays the options for managing the active file gallery. You should notice that the **Current Folder** heading at the top of the page displays **Packt Publishing** as a link, which is the title of our sample file gallery. You can switch to another folder by selecting the **Select Folder to Manage** button located at the top right-hand side of the page.

In order to upload a file, select the link titled **Upload File** located under the **Common Tasks** section to open the **File Management** page. You need to upload a file by clicking the **Pick File** button. A pop-up dialog box with the title **Upload File** will be displayed as shown in the screenshot overleaf. You can either upload a file from your system or specify the Uniform Resource Locator (URL) where the specified file resides. For our sample file gallery, we will upload a PDF file that is available locally.

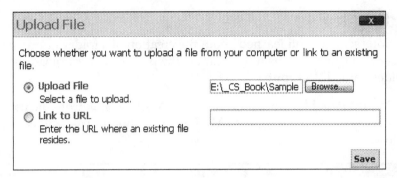

As soon as you click the **Save** button, the relevant file name will be displayed on the file editor page as shown in the following screenshot:

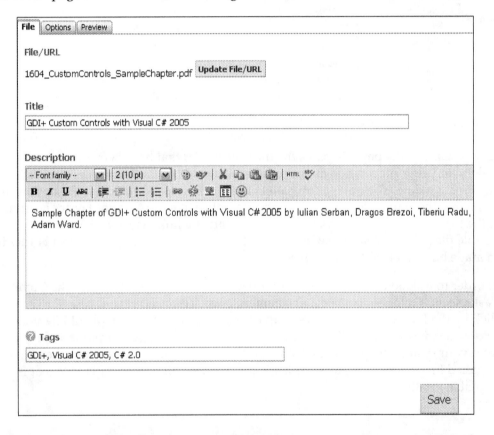

As you can see, we have supplied the required title and a short description for the uploaded file. We have also a entered few tags in the **Tags** field so that a search can be performed on the file gallery using these tags.

With the help of the **Options** tab, you can choose whether the specific file should be published or not. If disabled, files are not visible outside the **Control Panel**. By default, this option is enabled and we will keep it as such for our sample file gallery. The **Preview** tab can be used to view the title and description as they will appear inside the file gallery.

In a similar way, you can upload other files to the gallery. For our sample gallery, we will upload a PowerPoint presentation and a Word document as noted earlier. The files will be uploaded and added to the grid as shown below on clicking the **Save** button. The files will also be visible on the home page of the file gallery.

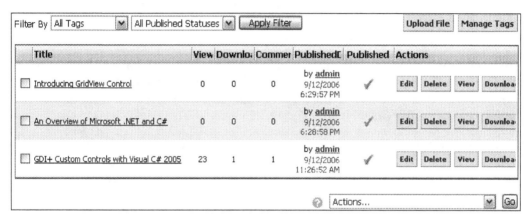

As you can see from the screenshot, you can directly upload a new file using the **Upload File** button, manage tags using the **Manage Tags** button, search for files using tags and the publication status options from the available **Filter By** drop-down list.

 You can also manage files by selecting the **Files** link located under the **Manage Content** section.

The Administrator can use the **Review Files** link to approve the publishing of files.

 Working with tags in a file gallery is similar to doing so in a photo gallery; you can refer to the *Managing Tags* section in this chapter.

# Working with Comments

As an Administrator, you can manage comments posted in the file gallery by your visitors. By default, all comments will be immediately published in the file gallery. If required, you can choose to approve them before publication. This can be done by selecting the **Review Comments** link from the **Files** section.

 In order to approve comments, you should enable comment moderation using the option **Moderate Comments** from the **Advanced File Settings** page located in the **Settings** panel.

Let us now post a comment to our sample file gallery. You will have to first log in to the Community Server as a user and click the link **Downloads** from the navigation bar. You will see a page displaying all the available files; select a file from the home page of the file gallery.

You will see a page with the title that we gave at the time of uploading the file. Scroll down to the page and enter the required comment. The **Web Site** field is optional. As soon as you click the **Add** button, a message box will be displayed stating that moderation is currently enabled.

After adding the comment, log in as Administrator and navigate to the **Review Comments** page, select the comment, and choose the option **Approve Selected Items** from the **Actions** drop-down box. The comment will be approved and visible in the gallery page of the relevant file.

Approved comments are automatically added to the grid on the **Comments** page located in the **Manage Content** section.

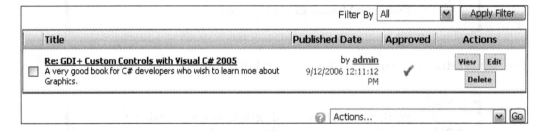

You can view, modify, and delete the comment using the appropriate buttons from the **Actions** column after selecting the relevant comment by clicking the appropriate checkbox. On clicking the **View** button, you will be directly taken to the relevant page to the file gallery and the comment can be viewed by scrolling down. You can also search comments based on their publication status using the options from the **Filter By** drop-down box.

# Managing Settings

You can manage some of the advanced settings using the options from the **Settings** section located on the left-hand side navigation panel. Let us examine each one of the options in detail:

## Title and Description

With the help of the options on this page, you can specify a title and description for the gallery. The title specified here will be displayed as a link on the **Current Folder** section in the middle of the **File Management** page.

## Advanced File Settings

You can modify and control the behavior of files within the active gallery with the help of this option. The settings included on this page are described below:

**Moderate Files**: If this is enabled, then the site Administrator needs to approve an uploaded file before it is visible in the gallery. This process can be done by selecting the **Review Files** link located under the **Common Tasks** section. By default, this setting is disabled.

**Enable File Notifications**: If enabled, owners of the specific folder will receive an email notification when a new file has been uploaded. By default, this setting is disabled.

**Enable Ratings**: If this is enabled, the uploaded files in a specific folder can be rated by registered users on a scale of 1 to 5. By default, this setting is enabled.

**Enable Comments**: If enabled, registered users can post comments about each individual file inside a specific folder. By default, this setting is enabled.

**Moderate Comments**: If this is enabled, the comments posted by users other than Administrators and moderators require approval prior to publication in the gallery. By default, this setting is disabled.

**Enable Comment Notifications**: If this is enabled, owners of the specific folder will receive an email notification as and when a new comment has been posted about a file inside the folder. By default, this setting is disabled.

## Advanced Syndication Settings

You can enable or disable RSS Syndication for the files inside the folder using the relevant setting on this page. You can also enable syndication for tags. By default all settings are enabled.

 Disabling a feed will not affect those users who have previously subscribed to the feed but it will still stop the feed from being displayed within the folder.

# Accessing the File Gallery

You can browse the file gallery using various methods. As an Administrator, you can directly access the relevant file in the gallery by clicking the **View** button from the grid on the **Files** page that appears on clicking the **Files** link under the **Manage Content** section. You can also navigate to the home page of the file gallery by clicking the link in the **Current Photo Gallery** section.

Your users can access the file gallery by clicking the **Downloads** link from the home page:

As you can see from the above screenshot, Community Server automatically uploads a sample file with the title **The Latest Community Server Licensing Guide** during the installation process. You can also see a list of all the files that we uploaded to our sample file gallery, which can be downloaded by selecting the **Download** button. As you can observe from the screenshot, the title of the file with most number of downloads is displayed in bold.

The numbers in the **Downloads** column corresponding
to each file will not be updated immediately after
downloading a file.

You will be able to view the details of each file on clicking the relevant title as
shown below:

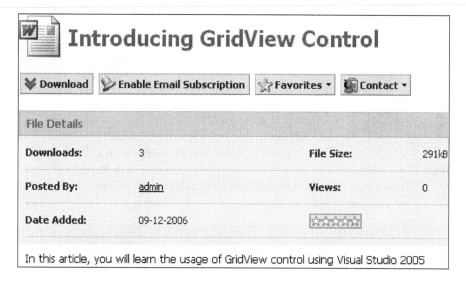

In order to download the Word file, you have to select the **Download** button.
Meanwhile, Administrators can directly manage a file in the gallery after signing into
the site as shown on the next page.

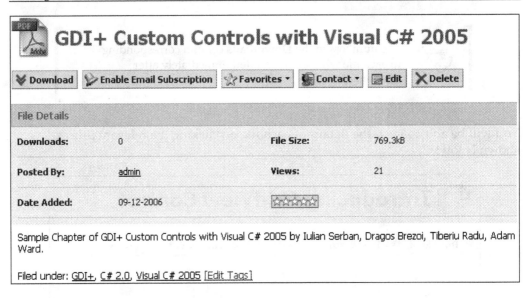

As you can see from the above screenshot, Administrators can modify or delete files in addition to managing other related tasks. They can also directly edit the tags using the **Edit Tags** link from each page inside the file gallery. When you click the **Edit Tags** link a pop-up dialog box will appear as shown below:

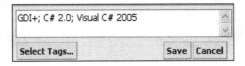

After entering the required tags, click the **Save** button to return to the file gallery page. If you click the **Select Tags** button, a pop-up dialog box will be displayed with a list of all the available tags.

# Viewing the Download Report

Community Server provides a facility to view the download report from the **Dashboard**.

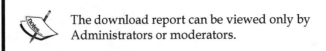

The download report can be viewed only by Administrators or moderators.

For this purpose, log in to the site as an Administrator and click the **Control Panel** link to move to the **File Management** page. Click the **My Files** link from the top navigation bar and select the **Files** link located under the **Manage Content** section. A grid will be displayed with a list of all files in the gallery, as shown below, along with a button captioned **Download(s) Report** on each row.

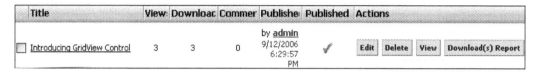

Clicking the **Download(s) Report** button displays a **Download Report** page that shows download information as shown below:

In order to instantly view the download report, you need to select the **Generate** button and a page as shown below will be displayed.

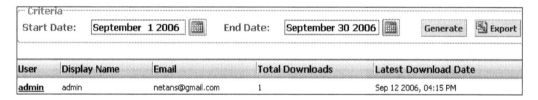

As you can see from the above screenshot, the file has been downloaded only once. It also shows the date on which the file was last downloaded.

Alternatively, you can download the report in Microsoft Excel Worksheet format by clicking the **Export** button. The extension of the downloaded Microsoft Excel Worksheet file is `.csv`. It stands for **Comma Separated Values** and is popularly used for generating reports.

# Summary

In this chapter, you learned about the creation and management of photo and file galleries using Community Server. You learned the various aspects involved with the help of sample photo and file galleries. You also learned the usage of each and every setting associated with the functioning of the galleries. The next chapter examines the working of the reader and roller functionality.

# 6
# Working with Reader and Roller

Nowadays, a lot of people maintain blogs about a wide range of content. These people can be your colleagues, family members, or friends. Sometimes, you may find that the blogs maintained by them are useful and you might like to keep a track of the content of their blogs. In such a situation, you will need a system by which you can combine and populate the posts into a common place, preferably your blog. Community Server comes with a powerful and robust features called **reader** and **roller**, with which you can monitor the content from each blog in which RSS feeds are available and display them either on your Community Server site or inside the homepage of your blog. The required content will be automatically pulled and displayed at regular intervals. In this chapter, we will examine the working of this feature with the help of feeds from blogs and websites.

## Overview

The reader feature can be used to display content from the RSS feeds. As an administrator, you can grant role-based access to reader for the members of your site. Reader is also called **Feed Reader** and looks very similar to bloglines in terms of focus and functionality.

Imagine that you are participating in a TechEd conference being conducted by Microsoft. Your local Microsoft office maintains a blog for each and every speaker. You need to display all the posts made by those speakers on their blogs, inside your Community Server site. Moreover, you also want to display information about the latest publications at `aspalliance.com`. With the help of roller, you can easily aggregate the content from various websites into your blog.

With the release of Community Server 2.1, roller functionality has been integrated with the blogs. Hence, all the content from the relevant RSS feeds will be aggregated and displayed inside the relevant blogs. This feature is called **Content Mirroring**. The core theory behind the working of roller is the RSS feeds generated by each blog. As you post each blog entry, its corresponding RSS feeds are also updated and hence the feeds in your website are also automatically updated upon refreshing. The forthcoming sections will examine the usage of reader and roller with the help of the feeds from the blogs and websites.

# Working with Reader

In order to work with the reader you should first add the required RSS feeds. For this purpose, log-in to the site as an administrator and select the **My Reader** link from the top navigation bar. Right-click the entry titled **My Feeds** and select **New Feed** as shown in the screenshot below:

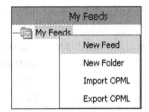

 By default, a site administrator will have permission to add feed URLs.

As soon as you click the entry, a pop-up dialog with the title **Add Feed** will be displayed. You need to enter the relevant RSS-feed URL as shown in the following screenshot:

As you can see, we have entered the feed address of Rob Howard's blog. In the same way, you can add the URLs of other feeds. For our sample reader, we will add the feed URL of Scott Guthrie's blog (`http://weblogs.asp.net/scottgu/rss.aspx`) and that of ASPAlliance (`http://aspalliance.com/rss.aspx`).

Clicking the **Add Feed** button will not display any content inside the reader. In order to display the content, you need to add the relevant feeds to the reader using **Aggregated Feeds** setting found inside the **Dashboard**.

# Aggregating Feeds

In order to aggregate the RSS feeds, select **Control Panel** link from the top navigation bar after logging into the site as an administrator. Locate the link titled **Manage feeds, control permissions, etc** from the **Reader Administration** section. The **Site Administration** page will be displayed. You will see a set of four options under the section **Reader** (see the following screenshot) on the left-side navigation panel.

 You can also grant role-based permissions for each registered user of the site to access the reader and manage the feeds. The users can post their own unique content from the **Reader Administration** section after logging into their site. We will examine this in more detail later on in this chapter.

Click the **Aggregated Feeds** link and select the **Add Feed** button inside the page. You will see a page titled **Add Aggregated Feed** as shown in the following screenshot:

ASPAlliance.com - Articles, reviews, and samples for .NET Developers (http://aspalliance.com/rss.aspx)
Rob Howard's Blog (http://weblogs.asp.net/rhoward/rss.aspx)
ScottGu's Blog (http://weblogs.asp.net/scottgu/rss.aspx)

\* = This feed appears to have errors. If you aggregate this feed you may not see any aggregated posts from it.

| Add Selected Feeds | Done |

As you can see, the list box displays a list of all feeds that we added using reader. As soon as you select the required feeds and click the **Add Selected Feeds** button, the feed URLs will be added inside the reader. You can also see the corresponding entries if you click the **Manage Feeds** link located under the the **Reader** section.

 You can select multiple feeds by pressing the *Ctrl* key along with the mouse click.

Let us now access the reader to examine the result. Click the link **Exit Control Panel and Return to Site** and select **My Reader** from the navigation bar on the top of the page. You need to expand **My Feeds** folder to view the feeds (see the screenshot below) that we added to the reader from the **Dashboard**.

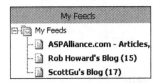

The **My Feeds** section shows how many posts are there on the homepage of the specific website or blog. The title of the relevant website or blog will be automatically populated as you can see from the above screenshot. As you select each feed, its corresponding posts will be displayed in two different sections as shown in the following screenshot:

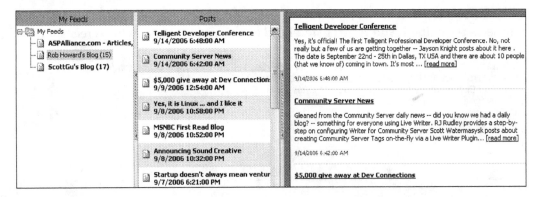

The middle section titled **Posts** displays a list of all posts pulled from the homepage of Rob Howard's blog along with the title, date, and time. The final column displays a detailed view of each post with an excerpt. You can read the post either by selecting the title of each post or by clicking the **read more** link found at the end of each excerpt. The relevant post will be opened in a new browser window.

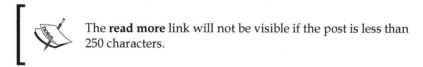

> The **read more** link will not be visible if the post is less than 250 characters.

Even if you delete a feed URL from the reader it will still appear on the **Aggregated Feeds** list box inside the **Dashboard**. This will enable you to add the deleted feed again to the reader as and when it is required.

# Managing Feeds

You can modify the feed URLs by clicking the **Manage Feeds** link. As soon as you click the link, you will view a page with the title **Manage User Feeds** with a grid, which will be populated with the relevant title, link, and the last updated time as shown in the following screenshot:

| Title | Link | LastUpdateDate | Actions |
|---|---|---|---|
| ScottGu's Blog | http://weblogs.asp.net/scottgu/default.a... | 9/14/2006 5:56:0... | Edit |
| ASPAlliance.com - Articles, reviews, and samples for .NET Devel... | http://aspalliance.com/ | 9/14/2006 5:56:0... | Edit |
| Rob Howard's Blog | http://weblogs.asp.net/rhoward/default.... | 9/14/2006 5:56:0... | Edit |
| 1 | | Page **1** of **1** (3 items) | |

Clicking the **Edit** button displays the **Feed Editor** page as shown in the following screenshot:

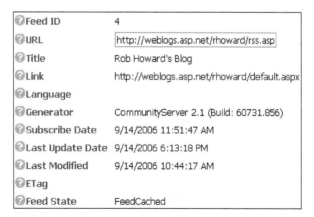

ETag is a part of the **Hyper Text Transfer Protocol (HTTP)** specification and is used in RSS feeds. You will find more information at `http://www.w3.org/Protocols/rfc2616/rfc2616-sec14.html#sec14.19` or `http://www.kbcafe.com/rss/rssfeedstate.html#entitytags`.

As you can see from the previous screenshot, most of the settings are read-only except for the URL field. You can modify the feed address by supplying a new URL in the field. The **Feed Editor** page shows the title of the blog along with the relevant dates. It also displays the current status of the feed in addition to the version and build number of Community Server.

# Granting Permissions for Users to Access the Reader

You can grant permissions to those users who require access to the feed reader. By default, only the site administrator can access the reader. But you can give permission to other registered users by granting access to them by using the options in the **Manage Roles** page. In order to view the page, you should click the **Manage Access** link from the reader section from the **Site Administration** page.

You should note that simply giving access to the registered users will not enable them to manage the reader. They can, however, view the reader by clicking the **My Reader** link from the top navigation bar. In order to give access to manage the reader you should grant role-based permissions by following the steps mentioned below:

1. Select the **Administration** link from the **Dashboard.**
2. Pull down the panel titled **Membership** from the navigation bar located on the left side.
3. Click the **Browse People** link and select a username from the grid on the **Member Search Results** page.
4. Select the **Add/Remove Roles** link from the **Roles** section on the **Profile** page.
5. Select the **ReaderAdministrator** and click the first arrow from the top to add the role to the specific user. In the same way, grant permission to the user for the reader user-role.
6. Click the **Save** button to finish the process and return to the **Profile** page.
7. Finally, apply the changes by clicking the **Save Changes** button located at the bottom of the profile page.

As soon as the registered users log in to the site, they can manage the reader by clicking the **Control Panel** link from the top navigation bar and selecting the **Manage feeds, control permissions, etc** link located under the **Reader Administration** section from the **Dashboard**.

# Working with Roller

As we examined earlier, the roller feature has been integrated with blogs. All the relevant content from the feeds will be visible either inside the blog's homepage on the site or on the specific blog in which you have enabled the feed. Let us now examine the working of roller in detail.

Firstly, pull down the **Blogs** section from the **Site Administration** page and select the **Blogs** link. A grid with a list of all blogs on the site will be displayed as shown in the screenshot below:

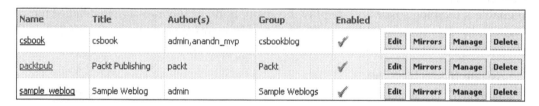

| Name | Title | Author(s) | Group | Enabled | | | | |
|------|-------|-----------|-------|---------|---|---|---|---|
| csbook | csbook | admin, anandn_mvp | csbookblog | ✓ | Edit | Mirrors | Manage | Delete |
| packtpub | Packt Publishing | packt | Packt | ✓ | Edit | Mirrors | Manage | Delete |
| sample_weblog | Sample Weblog | admin | Sample Weblogs | ✓ | Edit | Mirrors | Manage | Delete |

The functioning of roller is called the content mirroring. Hence, in order to add feeds to the blog roller, you need to select the **Mirrors** button. You will view a page titled **Mirror Feeds** with an empty grid. Selecting the **Add New Feed** button displays a pop-up dialog box. You should enter the required URLs and settings in the appropriate fields as shown in the next screenshot:

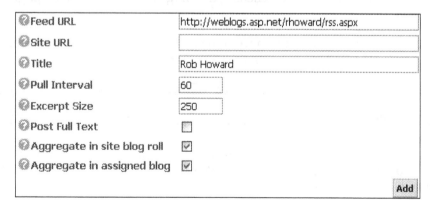

As you can see, we have specified to pull the posts from the blog maintained by Rob Howard. You can optionally specify the relevant site URL of the feed. We have also given a title for the feed so that you will know about the purpose of the feed at a later stage. Let us now examine the other settings in detail:

### Pull Interval

Community Server automatically checks for new posts from the specific feed URL based on the value on this field. The default value is 60 minutes. This means that any new posts to the related blog/website will be displayed on the blog roller after a gap of at most 60 minutes.

### Excerpt Size

This setting denotes the number of characters that should be displayed as an excerpt on the **Blog Roller** page. The default value is 250 characters. The excerpt will be truncated at the end of the first 250 characters.

### Post Full Text

If enabled, the blog roller will display the entire body of the message instead of the excerpt. By default, this setting is disabled and it means that an excerpt with 250 characters will be displayed along with a link to the original URL.

### Aggregate in site blog roll

If enabled, all the posts from the relevant feed will be displayed on the blog homepage of the site.

### Aggregate in assigned blog

If enabled, all the posts from the relevant feed will be displayed on the assigned blog homepage. For the purpose of our discussion, we have added a mirror feed to our sample blog — *csbook*. If this setting is enabled then you will be able to view all the relevant posts from the feed upon clicking the **Blogs** link from the homepage of our sample site.

As soon as you click the **Add** button from the pop-up dialog box, the required details will be added to the grid as shown in the following screenshot:

| Name | URL | Pull Interval | Last Pull | Actions | |
|------|-----|---------------|-----------|---------|--|
| Rob Howard | http://weblogs.asp.net/rhoward/rss.aspx | 60 | 9/15/2006 3:02:12 PM | Edit | Delete |

As you can see, the grid displays the name and URL that we entered and also other relevant settings. You can also modify and delete the feed using the appropriate button located under the **Actions** column.

You can view the relevant posts from the feed (see the following screenshot) if you navigate to the **Blogs** page of the relevant site to which the mirror feed has been added.

### Telligent Developer Conference

**0**
Comments
0 Views

Yes, it's official! The first Telligent Professional Developer Conference. No, not really but a few of us are getting together -- Jayson Knight posts about it here . The date is September 22nd - 25th in Dallas, TX USA and there are about 10 people...

09-14-2006, 8:18 PM from Rob Howard's Blog to Packt Publishing
Filed under: Community Server, Telligent

### Community Server News

**0**
Comments
0 Views

Gleaned from the Community Server daily news -- did you know we had a daily blog? -- something for everyone using Live Writer. RJ Rudley provides a step-by-step on configuring Writer for Community Server Scott Watermasysk posts about creating Community...

09-14-2006, 8:12 PM from Rob Howard's Blog to Packt Publishing
Filed under: Community Server, Telligent, Community, Live Writer

### $5,000 give away at Dev Connections

**0**
Comments
0 Views

So we were talking through promotions and advertising for the CodeSmith booth at Dev Connections in November . We had some really witty ideas for magazine ads (I'll refrain from telling you just how creative we got). But the more we thought about...

As you can observe from the above screenshot, the excerpt has been truncated, and you can view the complete content if you click the relevant title link. In the same way, you can add more mirror feeds to the relevant blog and all the posts will be aggregated and displayed as shown above.

# Managing Settings

You can modify the feed reader and blog roller options by using the **Settings** link located under the **Reader** panel inside the **Site Administration** page. Let us examine each one of the settings in detail.

**Last Modified Interval**

This setting is related to the feed reader. You can specify the time limit (in minutes) based on which the modified posts will be pulled. The default setting is two minutes. This means that the reader will automatically check for modified feed content on the relevant feeds once in every two minutes.

**Truncation Length**

You can specify the maximum length of characters for the blog content that should be displayed on the blog roller page. The default value is 500 characters.

Setting the value of the truncation length to zero displays
the whole body of each post on the homepage of the
blog roller.

### Page Size

You can specify the maximum number of results that should be displayed per
page on the **Blog Roller** page. The default value is 25 results. If you modify it to 100,
then roller will display 100 blog posts on the first page and then the posts will
be paginated.

### RSS Result Size

You can specify the maximum number of results that should be returned from the
RSS feed of the roller. The default value is 25 results.

# Summary

In this chapter, you learned how to work with reader and roller with the help of
sample feeds. We have examined the steps that have to be followed to configure
a reader. We also demonstrated how to grant role-based permissions for users
registered on the site to access and manage the reader. Towards the end of the
chapter, we have examined the required steps to set up the roller in addition to
important settings associated with reader and roller. In the next chapter, we will
learn how to manage members registered on the site.

# 7
# Managing your Community's Users

We have so far discussed the various applications included in Community Server, such as blogs, forums, galleries, reader and roller. The remaining chapters will focus on the management of members, customization, and generation of reports. In this chapter, you will learn how to manage the users that join your community and also some of the associated settings.

## The Community's Members

Members are truly the core of Community Server, because without members there wouldn't be a community! When enabled, people can join the community to post to blogs, forums, photos, files, and more. In most cases, you need not contact each and every member. But as your community's administrator, you will need to manage the settings associated with the members, such as approval of a new user registration and other related tasks. Sometimes, you will be required to search for a specific member and also to create new users internally. Community Server includes a separate area inside the administrator's **Dashboard** titled **Memberships**, with which you can, not only perform all these tasks, but also manage all the associated settings.

## Getting Started

In order to manage members, you should first log into the site as the administrator, and select the link titled **Control Panel** located on the top navigation bar. The Community Server **Dashboard** page will be displayed. This permission/ability to manage members can be delegated to other users later on and doesn't always require the administrator.

Select the link **Manage membership, roles, and user settings** located under the **Membership** section from the **Dashboard** page. The **Site Administration** page will be displayed with various options as shown below:

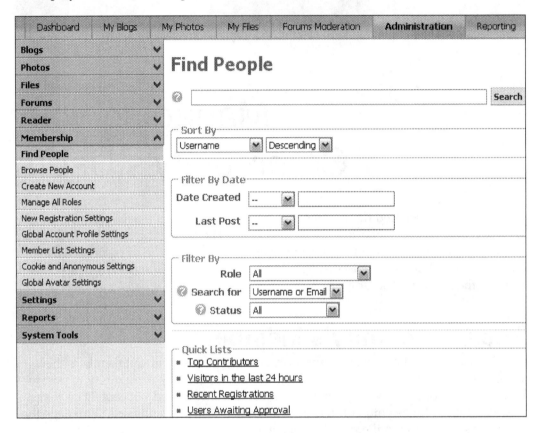

# Searching

As you can see from the above screenshot, the search functionality is initially displayed by default. You can search for members using different criteria such as their role or status. You can also refine the search using username, email address, number of posts, date of joining, and date on which the user was active on the site. Clicking the **Search** button without entering any options displays a page populated with all the registered users of your site as shown in the screenshot on the next page:

As your site grows, the number of users will increase. You can choose how many users should be displayed on the search results page by selecting the required option from the **Items per page** drop-down box, which is highlighted in the above screenshot.

You can also perform a search by selecting the required dates from the **Filter By Date** panel. You can either choose the date of creation of a post, or the date on which the last post was submitted on the site. First, you need to pick the relevant option from the **Date Created** drop-down box. Initially, the text fields are disabled. As soon as you select an option such as **On, After,** or **Before** from the relevant drop-down boxes, the Calendar control will be activated as shown in the screenshot shown below:

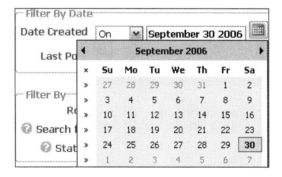

# Navigating Search Pages

As discussed above, the maximum number of entries that will be displayed on the member search results page is 20. Naturally, all the items from the 21st record will be displayed on the second page. The **Member Search Results** page includes a navigation bar at the bottom of the page as shown in the following screenshot. It will help you to swap between pages. You can either move forward or move backwards depending upon your requirements.

| Username | Email | Posts | Joined | Last Active | Actions |
|---|---|---|---|---|---|
| packt | anandn26@gmail.com | 0 | 9/5/2006 | 9/29/2006 | Actions |
| Anonymous | anonymous@localhost.com | 63 | 8/12/2006 | 9/30/2006 | Actions |
| anandn_mvp | communityserverbook@gmail.com | 5 | 8/31/2006 | 9/15/2006 | Actions |
| admin | netans@gmail.com | 33 | 8/12/2006 | 9/30/2006 | Actions |

Page 1 of 1 (4 items)

As you can see the above search result contains only one page, as we don't have more than 20 users. You can either use the scroll bar or the buttons with black colors to navigate between pages provided if you have more than 20 records in the search results.

When you drag the scroll bar the page number will be displayed. As soon as you stop scrolling, Community Server displays a screen titled **Loading** and after a while the desired page automatically appears on the screen.

# Examining Quick Lists Options

The **Find People** page displays a list of four link options under the title **Quick Lists** as shown in the following screenshot:

Quick Lists
* Top Contributors
* Visitors in the last 24 hours
* Recent Registrations
* Users Awaiting Approval

Let us now examine each one of the link options in detail:

# Top Contributors

Community Server displays a list of all registered users who have contributed posts on the site. This option will help you to track those users who make use of your site very often and also to reward them accordingly. By default, the page displays a list of all registered members on the site in descending order of their number of posts:

| Username | Email | Posts | Joined | Last Active | Actions |
|----------|-------|-------|--------|-------------|---------|
| Anonymous | anonymous@localhost.com | 63 | 8/12/2006 | 9/30/2006 | Actions |
| admin | netans@gmail.com | 33 | 8/12/2006 | 9/30/2006 | Actions |
| anandn_mvp | communityserverbook@gmail.com | 5 | 8/31/2006 | 9/15/2006 | Actions |
| packt | anandn26@gmail.com | 0 | 9/5/2006 | 9/29/2006 | Actions |

|◄   ◄  ▶  ▶|                                    Page 1 of 1 (4 items)

## Visitors in the Last 24 Hours

This option enables you to retrieve the username and other associated details of all those users who visited your site in the past 24 hours as shown in the following screenshot:

| Username | Email | Posts | Joined | Last Active | Actions |
|----------|-------|-------|--------|-------------|---------|
| admin | netans@gmail.com | 33 | 8/12/2006 | 9/30/2006 | Actions |

|◄   ◄  ▶  ▶|                                    Page 1 of 1 (1 items)

As you can see, the grid displays the username of the site administrator. This means that other registered users have not logged into the site in the last 24 hours.

## Recent Registrations

This option will display a list of all those users who registered recently on the site. In order to verify this, let us now log out as administrator and register on the site with a new username. After the successful creation of the users login as an administrator and click the link titled **Recent Registrations** from the **Quick Lists** panel. The grid at the bottom displays the details of the user who registered on the site after October 29, 2006:

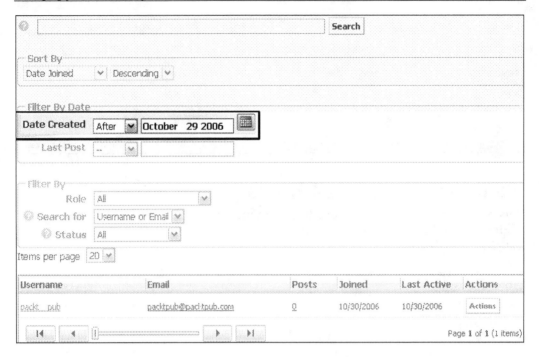

## Users Awaiting Approval

This option will display a list of all those users who registered on the site but require to be approved by the administrator. We have not enabled moderation of new registrations and hence if we click on the link no results will be displayed on the search results page.

Let us now examine how to moderate a new user registration. Locate the link titled **New Registration Settings** located under the **Memberships** panel. Select **Admin Approval** from the option titled **Account Activation** and click the **Save** button located at the bottom of the page.

 Refer to the *Managing Registration Settings* section for a detailed coverage of all the settings included in the **New Registration Settings** page.

After this, when a user registers on the site, the site administrator must approve the registration. We will now proceed to register a new user and examine the functionality. As soon as you submit the form after entering the required information, the following page will be displayed:

**Your account is pending approval**

Until your account is approved you will be unable to sign in. You will receive an email when your account has been approved.

In order to approve the registered user, you need to log in as an administrator and navigate to the **Control Panel**. Click the link located on the **Membership** panel and select **Users Awaiting Approval** from the **Quick Lists** section. The grid displays the details of the user who registered just now as shown below:

Select the username from the above screenshot and then select the **Approved** option and click the **Save Changes** button to approve the user.

As soon as the user is approved, an email confirming registration will be sent to the user.

You will be able to view the details of the approved user if you navigate to the **Recent Registrations** page as discussed in the previous section as shown below:

Selecting the **Actions** button will display a pop-up menu with which you can modify the password of the user, and add or remove roles. As an administrator, you can even delete a user by selecting the relevant option from the pop-up menu.

# Browsing All Members

As soon as you click on the link titled **Browse People** located under the **Membership** panel, a list of all registered members will be displayed as we have seen previously in this chapter. We have already discussed the various options on the page in the previous section. In this section, we will examine some of the hidden options on the page. As noted earlier, a pop-up menu will be displayed when you click the button captioned **Actions** as shown in the screenshot:

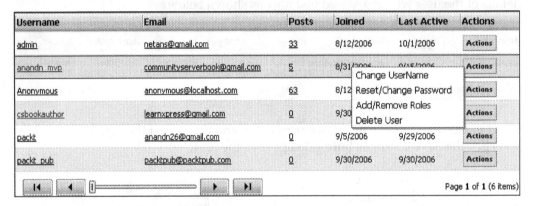

The above screenshot shows four options which enable you to modify the username and password of the specific user, add/remove roles, and also delete the user. Let us examine each of these options in detail.

# Modifying the Username

In order to modify the username of a member, you should select the **Change Username** option from the pop-up menu shown in the previous screenshot. This brings up the following dialog box:

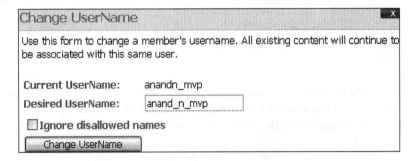

As you can see we have entered a new username in the **Desired UserName** field. As soon as you click the **Change UserName** button, the new username will be saved.

The updated username will appear on the grid (see screenshot) only if you refresh the page or click the **Browse People** link from the navigation panel.

| Username | Email | Posts | Joined | Last Active | Actions |
|---|---|---|---|---|---|
| admin | netans@gmail.com | 50 | 8/12/2006 | 10/30/2006 | Actions |
| anand_n_mvp | communityserverbook@gmail.com | 0 | 10/30/2006 | 10/30/2006 | **Actions** |
| Anonymous | anonymous@localhost.com | 65 | 8/12/2006 | 10/30/2006 | Actions |
| csbook_author | learn.xpress@gmail.com | 0 | 9/30/2006 | 9/30/2006 | Actions |
| packt | anandnC6@gmail.com | 0 | 9/5/2006 | 10/12/2006 | Actions |
| rob_howard | rob_here@gmail.com | 0 | 10/1/2006 | 10/1/2006 | Actions |

Page 1 of 1 (6 items)

# Changing Passwords

In order to modify the password of a member, you should select the **Reset/Change Password** menu item from the pop-up menu. A dialog box will be displayed where you should specify the new password for the specific member. You need to specify a new password twice and submit the form by clicking the **Change Password** button. The password will be immediately saved and you will be returned to the search page.

# Adding and Removing Roles

The core building block of Community Server is roles. They denote the permissions or rights granted by the site administrator to the specific member to manage the site. For instance, if you need to give a member the rights to manage the gallery then you should assign the role of *GalleryAdministrator* to the relevant member.

In order to add or remove roles for a specific user, you need to click the menu item **Add/Remove Roles** from the pop-up menu. The **User Roles** dialog will be displayed as shown overleaf:

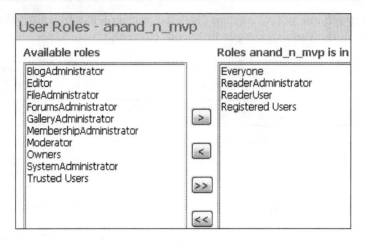

You can specify roles for the above user by selecting them from the **Available roles** list box and by using the arrow buttons on the middle of the dialog. The selected role(s) will be added to the list box on the right-hand side.

 You can select multiple roles by holding down the *Ctrl* key during the selection process.

For example, we will now examine how to give the role of **Moderator** to the selected user. Select **Moderator** from the **Available Roles** list box and click the first arrow (>). The selected role will be immediately added to the list box on the right-hand side (see the screenshot) and will be saved upon clicking the **Save** button.

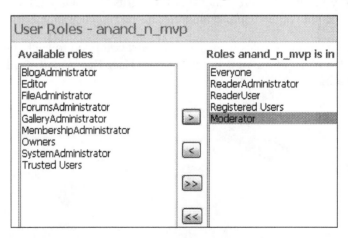

We have now given the status of **Moderator** to a member with the username **anand_n_mvp**. In the same way, you can specify roles for each user depending upon the requirements.

 The second arrow (<) from the top enables you to remove the selected role for the member. While the third arrow (>>) enables you to grant all the roles shown on the **Available Roles** section to the member irrespective of the selection, the fourth arrow (<<) removes all the roles granted to the member even if you haven't selected any roles from the list box.

# Deleting Users

As an administrator, you can delete a user from the site. This should be done as a last resort when the user performs any unacceptable act such as posting of unwanted messages or pictures. In order to delete the user, select the **Delete User** menu item from the pop-up menu. A dialog box will be displayed as shown below:

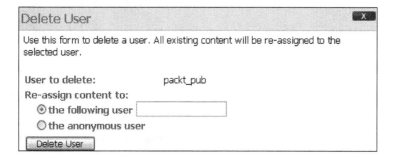

You should either assign all the existing content to another user on the site or to the anonymous user. The user will be then deleted from the system as soon as you click the **Delete User** button from the pop-up dialog box. The grid will be updated only if you either refresh the page or click the **Find People** link from the navigation panel.

# Creating a New Account

As an administrator, you can create a new member from within the **Membership** section inside the Control Panel. This feature will be useful if you would like to create a new member internally and want to restrict direct registration by members from the site.

In order to create an account for a member, select the **Create New Account** link located under the **Membership** section, enter the required information, and click the **Create User** button located at the bottom of the page.

As soon as you submit the page, the relevant username will be created if it doesn't exist and the **Find People** page will be displayed with a confirmation that the specified user has been successfully created.

# Managing Roles

You can globally manage the roles assigned to the various members with the help of the **Manage All Roles** link located under the **Membership** section.

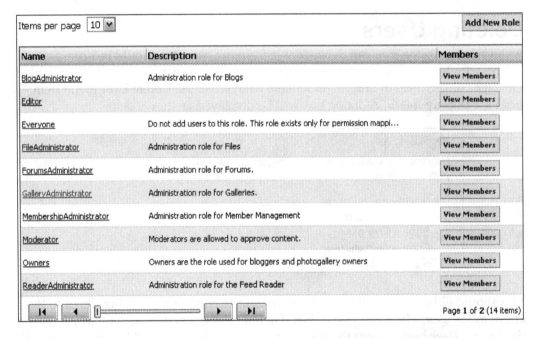

You can, not only add new roles, but also view a list of members who have been allocated a specific role. We will now examine for which users the site administrator has allocated *Moderator* status. Select the **View Members** button from the **Moderator** row.

As you can see from the above screenshot, the **Role** drop-down box displays the name of the role, which is moderator. There are currently two members who are assigned the status of moderator. In the similar way, you can display a list of all members who have been allocated various roles.

You can create new role by clicking the **Add New Role** button on top right-hand side of the **Manage All Roles** page. You need to enter the required information such as the **Name** and **Description** of the role in the **Edit Role** pop-up dialog box. You can also upload an icon, which will be displayed along with the posts (see screenshot below) submitted by the relevant member. As soon as you click on the **Save** button, the relevant role will be added to the system. Community Server assigns a unique ID for each role, which you can see by selecting the relevant role.

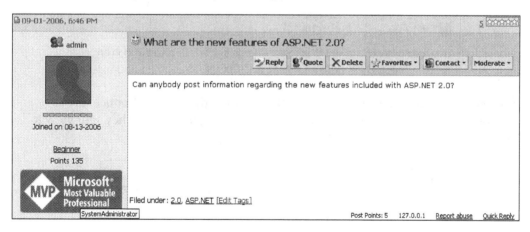

In order to associate an icon with an existing role, you should click the role and upload the icon by browsing for the image that has to be associated with the role.

# Managing Registration Settings

You can manage registration-related settings by selecting the link titled **New Registration Settings** located under the **Membership** section. With the help of the settings on the page, you can manage and control registration-related activities. Let us examine the usage of each of these settings in detail:

## Allow Login

If this is disabled, only administrators will be able to log in to the site. This setting is enabled by default and hence all users can log in.

## Allow Banned Users to Login

With the help of this option, you can control the activities of users who are banned in your site. By default, banned users are not able to log in to the site and they will view the following message when they attempt to log in to the site.

> **User Account Banned**
>
> You are no longer allowed to access the forums. If you believe this is in error, please check with the administrator(s) or moderator(s).

If banned users are allowed to log in to the site then they will not notice any considerable difference until they begin to post a blog or thread. They will view a message as shown below when they attempt to submit a post

> **User Banned**
>
> You have been banned from posting on the forums until 09-14-2158 3:19 PM. The reason for this ban is Other. Please return to participate in the forums after the ban has elapsed.

## Allow New User Registration

If this is disabled, or set to **No**, then new users can not register on the site. They will view a message as shown in the following screenshot, when they attempt to register on the site by selecting the **Join** link from the top of the site. This setting is enabled by default and hence users can register on the site at any time.

> **New User Registration Disabled**
>
> The administrator has disabled new account creation. Please check back later - or email the administrator - to see if it is possible to register.

# Show Contact Checkboxes

If this is enabled, users will see two settings, **Allow this site to contact me** and **Allow this site's partners to contact me**, at the bottom of the **Site Options** tab when editing their profile. Your users will also see these two options on the registration form page when they signup on the site by clicking the **Join** link located on the top of the site. These settings are disabled by default. Your users will receive communications from the site and its partners depending upon these settings.

# New User Moderation Level

With the help of this option administrators can moderate new posts made by the users. If you select the option **User is Moderated** the site administrator should approve the post submitted by the relevant user before publishing it on the site.

# Username Regular Expression Pattern

This setting provides a regular expression pattern based on which usernames are created. Community Server rejects the registration of those users who do not follow the specified pattern while entering usernames. The default pattern is **[a-zA-Z]+[^\<\>]*** and it implies that a string should begin with at least one letter (a-z of upper or lower case) followed by any characters other than < or >.

# Username Minimum Length

With the help of this setting, you can specify the minimum length that should be entered for usernames. The default value is 3. The registration setting will not accept a username if it is less than 3 characters and will display an error message that prompts the user to use a username with more than 3 characters.

# Username Maximum Length

With the help of this setting, you can specify the maximum length that should be entered for usernames. The default value is 64. The registration setting will not accept a username if it is more than 64 characters and will display an error message that prompts the user to use a username with less than 64 characters.

# Account Activation

This setting specifies how an account or a new registration should be activated. If **Automatic** is selected then Community Server will immediately approve the registration. If **Admin Approval** is selected then an administrator should approve the registration before the relevant user can work on the site. We have already discussed this setting previously in this chapter.

# Password Recovery

Users often forget the password that they either supplied during registration or modified at a later stage. This handy setting specifies the manner in which the password should be recovered. There are two different ways by which a user can recover the password. They are **Reset** and **Link**.

If **Reset** is selected, Community Server will automatically recover the password if the username matches with the one in the database. The recovered password will be emailed to the user. On the other hand, if the value **Link** is selected then the specific user will receive an email with a link. The password will be restored upon clicking the link and entering a new password twice.

# Password Regular Expression Pattern

This setting provides a regular expression pattern based on which passwords are created and stored. Community Server rejects the registration of those users who do not follow the specified pattern while entering their password. The default pattern is **(.\*)** and it implies that you can supply any string as your password. But depending on the regular expression (regex) options the newline character may not be matched. There are no hardcore restrictions for passwords as it is ultimately the choice of users to protect themselves from hackers.

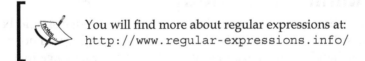

You will find more about regular expressions at:
`http://www.regular-expressions.info/`

# Managing Account Profile Settings

You can manage the profile-related settings of users by selecting the link titled **Global Account Profile Settings** located under the **Membership** section. With the help of the options on the page, you can manage signatures, gender, and theme-related settings. Let us examine the usage of each of these settings in detail:

# Allow Signatures

If this is disabled then your users will not be able to add or edit signatures in their profile. This feature will not be available until you enable it from the administrator Control Panel. By default this setting is enabled. It is not a good idea to disable this feature as users may include signatures along with the posts.

 A signature mainly includes the name, designation, and relevant URLs of the web sites managed by users. It can also contain images.

# Enable Signatures

If this is enabled, signatures are displayed at the bottom of each post as shown in the following screenshot:

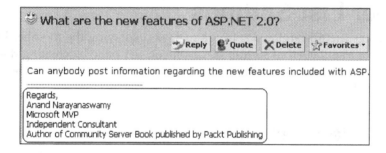

# Signature Maximum Length

This setting enables you to specify the maximum number of characters that is allowed for signatures. The default value is 256. You can increase this limit if you wish but it will be optimum if it is maintained below 500 characters.

# Allow Gender

With the help of this setting, administrators can enable the gender functionality on the site. This feature is mainly used in forums. The relevant gender icon will be displayed along with all posts made by that user.

After enabling the setting, click on the username link located on the top of the site and navigate to the tab titled **About**. Select a value from the option titled **Gender** and click the **Save Changes** button.

In order to view the gender icon, browse to any of the posts on the forum. You can view the gender icon on the left side of each post. In order to view an icon for a female user you need to modify the profile accordingly by setting the value of the **Gender** property to female.

## Enable User Theme Selection

If this is enabled, users can select an appropriate theme that overrides the default theme for their site.

## Require Authentication for Profile Viewing

If this is enabled anonymous users cannot view the profile of other registered users without logging into the site. This option will force them to log in if they are not logged in.

# Member List Settings

You can manage member-related settings such as displaying the member list, and the total number of members that should be displayed per page by clicking the **Member List Settings** link located under the **Membership** section. Let us examine each of the options in detail:

## Display Member List

If this is enabled, users can view a list of all members registered on the site. This setting is enabled by default.

## Enable Advanced Member Searching

If this is enabled, users can make use of symbols for performing complex searches on the site. Some of the popular symbols used while searching are AND, OR, and +.

## Enable Audit Counters

If this is enabled, audit counters are displayed as a new column in the list members. Users can view the counter when they navigate the members page. This setting will work only if **Display Member List** option has been enabled by the administrator.

# Members per Page

With the help of this option, you can specify the total number of members that should be displayed per page when a user performs a search operation. By default the value is 20.

# Managing Cookie and Anonymous Settings

You can manage cookie and anonymous user-related settings by selecting the link titled **Cookie and Anonymous Settings** located under the **Membership** section. Let us examine each of the settings in detail:

## Roles Cookie Enabled

Community Server generates an HTTP cookie that is used to store an encrypted string containing user roles. This setting is enabled by default.

## Track Anonymous Users

With the help of this setting, you can track the Internet Protocol (IP) address of anonymous users. Anonymous users are those users who are not signed into the site. As an administrator you need to keep a strict watch on these users so that you can check whether they are abusing the forum. Community Server records the IP address of each anonymous user, with which you can track their destination.

## Roles Cookie Name

This setting enables you to specify a name for the cookie that is used to store user roles. As noted earlier, the management of members is done using roles and they are stored internally on the user's system under the default name, which is **CSRoles**.

## Roles Cookie Expiration

This setting specifies the time limit after which the roles cookie will expire after its initiation. The default value is 20 minutes.

# Anonymous Cookie Name

You can specify a name for the cookie that is used for anonymous users. The default name is **CSAnonymous**.

# Anonymous Cookie Expiration

This setting specifies the time limit after which the cookie is set for anonymous users will expire after its initiation. The default value is 20 minutes.

# Cookie Domain

You can specify the part of a domain name such as *domainname.com* that will be used for storing the cookie. The default value for this setting is **localhost**. The actual domain name for the cookie in a local environment will be *Cookie:System-Name@localhost/*.

The above-mentioned name can be accessed by navigating to the **Tools | Internet Options** menu of your browser. We assume that you are using Internet Explorer. You need to click the **Settings** button and you will see the **Settings** dialog box. Click the **View Files** button to view the generated cookies. You will need to delete all existing cookies and browse the site from the beginning to see the real effect behind the generation of cookies.

# Anonymous User Online Window

You can set the time interval for tracking the total number of anonymous users who are accessing the site using this setting. The default value is 30 minutes. This means that Community Server will automatically display the usernames of those anonymous users who accessed the site in the last 30 minutes.

# Managing Avatar Settings

You can manage avatar-related settings by selecting the **Global Avatar Settings** link located under the **Membership** section. In forum parlance, an avatar means any graphical image that a user might use to identify them, generally a photograph or logo. It uniquely identifies your line of business. For instance, if you are the CEO of a web hosting company then you can display a logo of your company so that users can recognize you from your firm. Moreover, you can also showcase your logo. For example, if you are a Microsoft MVP then you can display any one of the logos supplied by Microsoft as your avatar as shown next:

# Enable Avatars

If this is enabled, your users can make use of the avatar feature and can display their identity as described in the previous section. This setting will work only if it has been enabled by the user from the **Avatar** tab on their profile (see the screenshot below). The users will be required to upload the image that will be displayed as their avatar along with their posts. They can modify the avatar by simply browsing for the image and selecting the **Update** button.

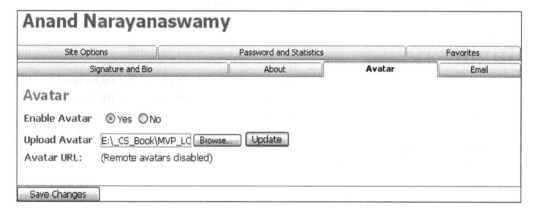

# Enable Remote Avatars

If this is enabled, your users can make use of a remote image as their avatar instead of browsing for an image from their local hard drive. The images will be preferably hosted on an external website or on the same website depending upon the circumstances. This setting is disabled by default for both site administrator and users and will be available for registered users only if it has been enabled by the administrator.

Once the administrator has enabled remote avatars, users can specify the URL in the **Avatar URL** field from the profile page as shown below:

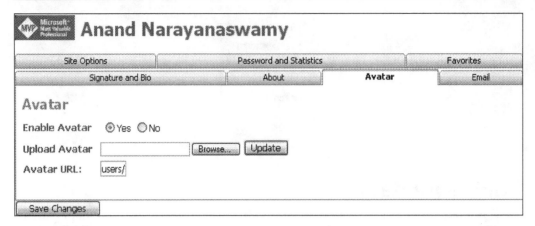

## Avatar Dimensions

This setting enables you to specify the dimension with which the avatar will be displayed on the site. By default, the value of this setting is 80x80. However, you can modify the values according to your requirements.

## Summary

Effective management of members is a must for any site serving the community. This statement is absolutely true for Community Server as it provides a robust mechanism for searching and managing members for administrators and moderators. This chapter examined all the settings for the effective management of your members in addition to the management of avatars. The next chapter will examine about the various options available for customizing Community Server.

# 8
# Customizing Community Server

In this chapter, we will demonstrate how to modify the look and feel of your site with the help of themes. You will also learn how to customize themes with the help of Cascading Style Sheet (CSS) files. We will go one step further ahead and examine the implementation of the FreeTextBoxWrapper add-on and calendar module into Community Server site. Towards the end of the chapter, you will learn how to create custom links on the navigation bar.

## Customizing the Home Page

In order to customize the home page, you should first log in as a user with site administration privileges. Firstly, we will examine how to modify the header area, which includes the headings and logo. We will also examine how to modify the default content on the home page.

## Modifying Headings and Logos

You can modify the top heading and its sub-heading by clicking on the respective content and entering new text. However, you can also modify them by clicking the **Site Name & Description** link located inside the **Settings** panel on the **Site Administration** page.

The site logo can be modified by replacing the image titled `title.gif` located under the `Themes\default\images\Common` folder with a new image. We would suggest you to create a new image and give its name as `title.gif`. You can then rename the original image with any other name and place the new image inside the above-mentioned folder. You need to refresh the site for the new logo to appear on the site.

# Editing Content

By default, a welcome message is displayed along with a short introduction about Community Server on the home page of the site. The page also features images of showcased sites and also some relevant links for obtaining documentation and support. In order to modify this content, you just need to place your mouse cursor over it and double-click on it. As soon as you double-click, a text editor opens up populated with the home page content. You can then format the content by inserting images, hyperlinks, and emoticons, and using the various options available in the editor. Finally, click on the **Save Changes** button to save and return to the home page. Your new content will automatically appear on the home page.

# Modifying the Theme of your Site

You can change the look and feel of your site with the help of various themes included with Community Server. Each theme consists of several individual skin files, which consist of related user controls and Cascading Style Sheets (CSS). With the release of Community Server 2.1, themes are controlled by style sheet rather than user controls as was the case in previous versions. We will discuss how to modify themes using CSS files in the *Modifying Themes* section.

In this section, we will examine how to modify the appearance of your site using the themes included with Community Server. By default, Community Server includes three themes, which you can use to change the look and feel of your site.

You can separately download and install themes available either at the official site at http://communityserver.org/files/folders/themes_and_skins/default.aspx or from third-party vendors and developers. You should only install those themes that are designed for Community Server 2.1. However, you can convert themes meant for Community Server 2.0 and implement them for your Community Server 2.1 installation by following the steps mentioned at http://getben.com/archive/2006/08/08/Updating-CS2.0-Themes-for-CS2.1.aspx.

In order to modify the theme for the whole site, click on the username link at the top of the home page and select the **Site Options** tab. Locate the **Theme** drop-down list and change its value either to **basic blue** or **alternate1**. For the purpose of our discussion we will modify its value to **basic blue** and you will be able to view the modified site immediately after clicking the **Save Changes** button. The following screenshot shows the blogs home page decorated with the basic blue theme.

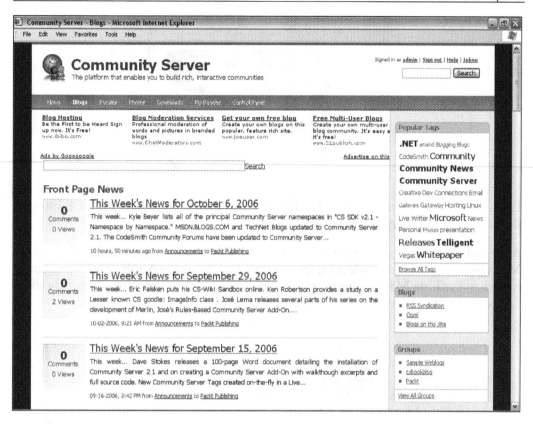

If you have installed any third-party themes then they will also be populated inside the **Theme** drop-down list.

# Modifying the Theme of your Blog

Let us now examine how to modify the appearance of blogs by using various themes. As explained in Chapter 3 *Working with Blogs*, you can manage all the blogs on the site as an Administrator. For this purpose, click the **Control Panel** link and select the **My Blogs** link. You will view the **Blog Management** page. Pull the **Global Settings** panel and select the **Change How My Blog Looks** link located under it. You can modify the appearance of your blog by selecting the appropriate theme from the **Theme** drop-down box. As soon as you select a theme, its corresponding preview will be displayed as shown in the following screenshot, so that you can choose another if it doesn't suit your needs.

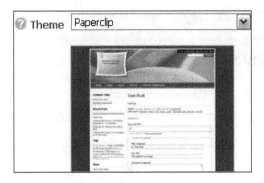

The appearance of your blog will be changed as soon as you click the **Save** button at the bottom of the **Blog Management** page.

As an Administrator, you can switch between blogs by clicking the **Select Blog to Manage** button and then selecting the relevant link from the **AppKey** column. You will view the **Blog Management** page for the selected blog and you can modify its theme as explained earlier.

>  As an Administrator, you can globally modify the theme for all blogs on the site by selecting the appropriate theme from the **Default Theme** drop-down list from the **Default Presentation** link located under the **Blogs** section inside the **Site Administration** page

Members can change the theme for their blogs by selecting the **My Blog Dashboard** page located under the **Common Tasks** section from the home page of their respective blogs. In order to access this link, members should browse their blog by using the actual Uniform Resource Locator (URL) such as `http://localhost/cs21/blogs/csbook/default.aspx`.

# Modifying Themes

In the previous sections, you have learned how to modify the look and feel of your site using themes. In this section, we will examine how to modify the themes included with Community Server.

Each theme consists of several folders, namely images, Masters, Skins, and style. The style folder contains several Cascading Style Sheet (CSS) files, which you need to modify in order to change the appearance of the active theme. For instance, in order to change the background color, you should modify the relevant property from the appropriate Cascading Style Sheet (CSS) file.

In order to modify the appearance of the home page, you need to open the Common. css file located inside Style folder of the corresponding theme and update the relevant property with the correct value.

For instance, if you would like to change the background color for your site, you need to open the Common.css file located under Themes\default\style folder and modify the background-color property located under the body, html section by supplying the appropriate color code as shown below:

```
body, html
{
    margin: 0px;
    padding: 0px;
    color: #000000;
    font-family: Tahoma, Arial, Helvetica;
    background-color: #999966;

}
```

> You can obtain the correct color codes for each specific color from http://html-color-codes.com/.

We assume that you are using the theme named **default**. In the same way, you can modify the background color of other themes by opening the CSS file located inside the style folder of the corresponding theme.

You can also modify the background color of the page header and other adjoining areas by supplying the appropriate value for the background-color property located in the #Common class as shown below:

```
#Common
{
    background-color: #3399CC;
    border-top: solid 6px #bbde79;
}
```

If you need to change the appearance of the forum home page for the theme named default, then you should open the forum.css file located in the Themes\default\style folder.

# Modifying Themes Dynamically

Site Administrators will have access to the file system and hence they can directly modify the CSS files as discussed above. However, registered users do not have FTP access and hence cannot modify the theme for their blog. For the benefit of users, Community Server includes a feature to provide the required style tags from within the **Dashboard**.

In order to perform this task, click the **Control Panel** link from the home page and select the **My Blogs** link from the **Blog Management** page. Click the **Change How My Blog Looks** link located in the **Global Settings** section, select the **CSS Overrides** tab and supply the appropriate code for the corresponding style ID as shown below:

```
#Common
{
    background-color: yellow;
}
```

We have now modified the color of the header and other adjoining areas of the current blog's home page. You can view the output by clicking the link beside the **Current Blog** section from the **Blog Management** page. As you can see, we have modified the theme without opening any CSS files.

# Working with Add-ons

You can further enhance the working of your site with the help of add-on packages that are available from the official website (http://www.communityserver.org) of Community Server. You should note that a majority of these packages are associated with the previous versions of Community Server and you should install only those packages that are developed for Community Server 2.1.

The installation instructions are provided along with each add-on package and you should refer to them to cross-check for compatibility of the add-on with the Community Server version you are using. You should always take a backup of all the existing files before installing any add-on packages so that you can restore the site if there is any problem during the installation process.

You can integrate powerful functionalities such as windows, passport, forms, and cookie authentication on your site. In addition to these, you can also implement features such as enterprise search, news gateway, and FTP server on your site using the relevant add-on packages. It is beyond the scope of this chapter to examine each one of these packages. You will find more information regarding the steps to be followed to work with these add-on packages at: `http://docs.communityserver.org/`

Add-on packages enhance a site with advanced functionalities such as adding an advanced textbox editor, Google Sitemap, and much more. As of writing this book, the **Downloads** section lists only two add-on packages for Community Server 2.1. The one that is commonly used is a textbox editor called **FreeTextBoxWrapper**. It is a robust, powerful, and free editor, which contains many features that are not available with the editors shipped with Community Server. Let us discuss about the installation and usage of **FreeTextBoxWrapper** control add-on.

# Using FreeTextBoxWrapper Control

Community Server contains three different content editors that let you post content to your site namely: **Plain Text**, **Standard**, and **Enhanced**. But these editors don't provide advanced functionalities such as formatting source code, managing images, etc. These features are provided by a third-party content editor called FreeTextBoxWrapper. The **FreeTextBoxWrapper** content editor is developed by George J. Capnias and is available for download at `http://communityserver.org/files/folders/add-ons/default.aspx`.

In order to download the control, you need to log in as a member and navigate to the **Downloads** section by clicking its link from the top navigation bar. Expand the tree titled **Community Downloads** and select the **Add-on** folder as shown below:

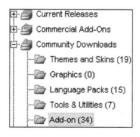

As soon as you click the link, you will see a list of all add-on files on the right-hand side of the page. You have to locate the link titled **FreeTextBoxWrapper for Community Server v2.1 series**. After locating the link, you need to select it and click the **Download** button at the top of the page to download the required file in ZIP format. The extracted file consists of different folders meant for various builds of Community Server. Each folder contains the required Dynamic Link Library (DLL) files for both .NET 1.1 and 2.0.

# Installing the FreeTextBoxWrapper Control

Before beginning to work with the control, you should install it properly. Firstly, you should find out the version of Community Server you have installed. For this purpose, click the **Control Panel** link and scroll down to the bottom of the **Dashboard** page. You will find the version number on the right-hand side of the page (**2.1.60809.935**, in our case).

As noted earlier, the textbox control ships with DLL files for the various builds of Community Server 2.1. You should use the files available inside the v1.1.4322 folder located inside the 2.1.60809.935 folder. If you have installed Community Server on .NET Framework 2.0 then you should use the files inside the folder v2.0.50727. Follow the steps given below to install **FreeTextBoxWrapper** control:

1. Copy the DLL files located inside the folder mentioned above and paste them to the bin folder located inside your Community Server site.

2. Copy the FreeTextBox3 folder and the contents of the Themes folder from the unzipped folder, CommunityServer[1].FreetextBoxWrapper.2006-08-15, and paste them to the root of your Community Server site.

3. Finally, open the CommunityServer.txt file and copy the provided code from the <editors> section to the <editors> section of CommunityServer.config file located in the root directory of your Community Server site.

The <editors> section should finally appear as shown in the listing given below:

```
<editors>
  <editor name="FreeTextBox Standard" skinName="Skin-Editor-FTB.ascx"
  default="true" />
  <editor name="FreeTextBox Enhanced" skinName="Skin-Editor-
  FTBEnhanced.ascx" />
  <editor name="Plain Text" skinName="Skin-Editor-PlainText.ascx" />
  <editor name="Standard" skinName="Skin-Editor-Standard.ascx"/>
  <editor name="Enhanced" skinName="Skin-Editor-Enhanced.ascx" />
</editors>
```

You have successfully installed the **FreeTextBoxWrapper** control. In order to work with the editor, you should reload the site and modify the value of the **Content Editor** drop-down list located inside the **Site Options** tab from the profile page.

 In order to access the profile page, click the username link at the top of the site.

As you can see, the **FreeTextBox** control includes two different options: **FreeTextBox Standard** and **FreeTextBox Enhanced**. The **Enhanced** editor provides features such as code formatting and an image gallery, which are not available with the **Standard** editor. For the purpose of our discussion, we will select the **FreeTextBox Enhanced** option and click the **Save Changes** button located at the bottom of the page.

You have now chosen to use **FreeTextBox Enhanced** as your editor for the whole site. Hence, you can see the editor if you try to submit a post to your blog or forums, or in any other location where user input is required.

Let us now examine some of the features of the editor by submitting a post to the **ASP.NET 2.0** forum, which we created earlier. For this purpose, click the **Forums** link, select the relevant forum from the home page and click the **Write a New Post** button. You will see a blank page powered with a rich toolbar as shown below:

As you can see from the above screenshot, the editor includes more functionalities than the other editors included within Community Server.

You can insert the current time by using the yellow color clock icon. It is now possible to insert symbols by using the relevant options from the **Symbols** drop-down list. You can also insert images from the gallery included within the editor. Moreover, you can also insert content from the file and photo galleries by using the **Select Content** icon from the editor toolbar.

Let us now examine how to insert and format a sample C# code snippet. Firstly, select the **Insert Code Snippet** icon and enter or paste the required code in the pop-up window as shown in the screenshot in the next page.

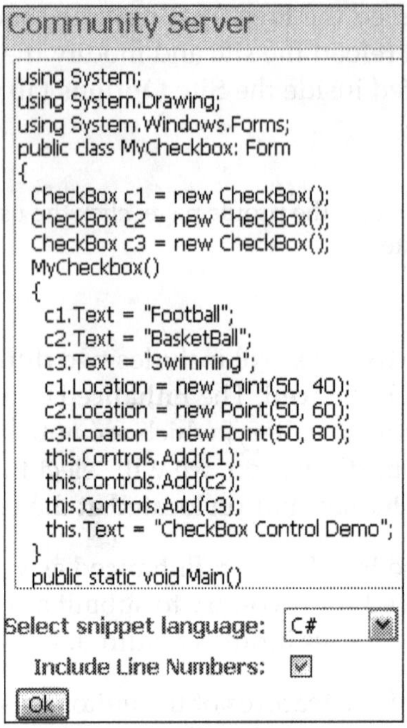

```
Community Server

using System;
using System.Drawing;
using System.Windows.Forms;
public class MyCheckbox: Form
{
  CheckBox c1 = new CheckBox();
  CheckBox c2 = new CheckBox();
  CheckBox c3 = new CheckBox();
  MyCheckbox()
  {
    c1.Text = "Football";
    c2.Text = "BasketBall";
    c3.Text = "Swimming";
    c1.Location = new Point(50, 40);
    c2.Location = new Point(50, 60);
    c3.Location = new Point(50, 80);
    this.Controls.Add(c1);
    this.Controls.Add(c2);
    this.Controls.Add(c3);
    this.Text = "CheckBox Control Demo";
  }
  public static void Main()
```

Select snippet language:   [ C# ▼ ]

Include Line Numbers:   [✓]

[ Ok ]

As you can see from the above screenshot, we have enabled the **Include Line Numbers** checkbox. This feature inserts numbers on each line so that you can reference them while discussing the code. The final output of our sample code snippet will appear as shown in the screenshot opposite.

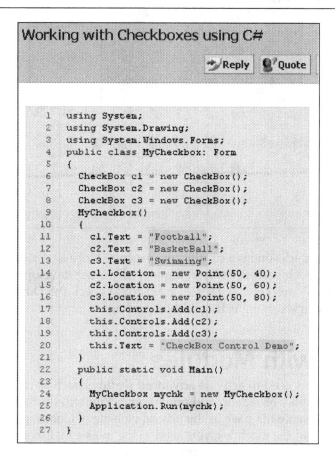

You will observe that the code has been formatted nicely with different colors and line numbers. Similarly, you can format code snippets of other languages such as VB.NET, J#, T-SQL, and ASP.NET. You can even format Microsoft Intermediate Language (MSIL) and JavaScript code.

Another interesting feature of the **FreeTextBox** control is that it has an enhanced emoticon viewer as shown overleaf.

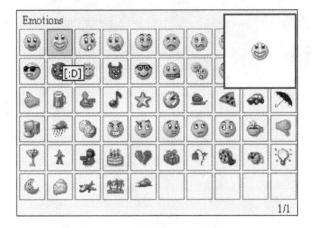

The development of add-ons is a continuous process. More and more new add-on packages will be developed either by Telligent or by other developers and will be added to the **Downloads** section. Hence, you should check the **Downloads** area frequently for any updates regarding add-on packages.

# Working with Modules

Modules are plug-ins used to activate advanced features such as tagging events on the calendar, display of videos, and much more. You will find a list of available modules on the **Downloads** page at the official website of Community Server. In order to download the modules, you need to log in as a member at http://www.communityserver.org and navigate to the **Downloads** section by clicking its link from the top navigation bar. Expand the tree titled **Community Downloads** and select the **CSModules** folder.

In this chapter, we will discuss the implementation and usage of the **DanBartels. CS.Calendar** module. The main function of this module is that it lets you tag your posts so that their titles show on a community calendar for your site. This module is extremely useful if you plan to host several meetings and events either for your company or for your user group.

An add-on is a business rule or other compiled code that adds specific functionality; for example the single sign-on libraries are 'add-ons'. A module is a business rule or other compiled code that handles events raised by Community Server and implements the base class or interface derived from a Community Server module.

Firstly, download the **DanBartels.CS.Calendar** module in ZIP format by locating the **DanBartels.CS.Calendar** module. After extracting the file follow the steps given below to integrate the module into your site.

1. Add the contents of the `bin`, `Calendar`, `Themes`, and `Utility` folders into the root of your Community Server site.

2. Add the contents of the `communityserver.merge.config` file to the `communityserver.config` file located inside the root of your Community Server site.

3. Add the contents of the `SiteUrls.merge.config` file to the `SiteUrls.config` file located inside the root of your Community Server site.

We would suggest you to add the following tag as a final item inside the `<navigation>` element so that the relevant link will be placed at the end of the other links on the navigation bar.

```
<link name="calendar" resourceUrl="calendarhome" text="Calendar" />
```

Once you finish the above mentioned steps, you need to update the changes in the `web.config` file by opening it using Notepad and saving the file. You will notice that a new module named **Calendar** has been added on the navigation bar immediately after refreshing the site as shown below:

| **Home** | Blogs | Forums | Photos | Downloads | My Reader | Control Panel | Calendar |
|----------|-------|--------|--------|-----------|-----------|---------------|----------|

We have successfully integrated the **Calendar** module inside Community Server. The next step is to examine the usage of the module. In order to perform this task, you need to simply add the tag similar to `[cal]10-20-2006[/cal]` anywhere in the body of the editor while writing a post. The resulting link will appear on the calendar as shown in the screenshot below:

| ◀ | | | October 2006 | | | ▶ |
|---|---|---|---|---|---|---|
| Sunday | Monday | Tuesday | Wednesday | Thursday | Friday | Saturday |
| 1 | 2 | 3 | 4 | 5 | 6 | 7 |
| 8 | 9 | 10 | 11 | 12 | 13 | 14 |
| 15 | 16 | 17 | 18 | 19 | 20 Trivandrum .NET User Group Meeting | 21 |

As you can observe from the above screenshot, a new link has been added with the relevant title against the date **October 20, 2006** and clicking on it will take you to the relevant post on the site. Hence, you can infer that the **Trivandrum .NET User Group Meeting** is scheduled to be held on that date. In the same way, you can add other events and each one of them will appear on the calendar according to their date of occurrence.

# Creating Custom Links

You can create your own links on the navigation bar by simply inserting the code as given below inside the `<navigation>` element in the `SiteUrls.config` file located at the root of your Community Server site.

```
<link name="Microsoft" navigateUrl="http://www.microsoft.com/"
text="Microsoft" />
<link name="Learnxpress" navigateUrl="http://www.learnxpress.com/"
text="Learnxpress" />
```

After saving the `SiteUrls.config` file, open and then save the `web.config` file and navigate to your site. You will see two links captioned **Microsoft** and **Learnxpress** as shown below:

| Home | Blogs | Forums | Photos | Downloads | Calendar | Microsoft | Learnxpress |
|------|-------|--------|--------|-----------|----------|-----------|-------------|

Clicking on these links will enable you to navigate to the websites pointed to by their `navigateUrl` property.

# Summary

In this chapter, you learned about the different ways in which you can customize the appearance of your Community Server site. We have also shown you the different ways its which you can modify the appearance of your site and blog using themes including their customization aspects. Towards the end of the chapter, you learned about the implementation and usage of the **FreeTextBoxWrapper** add-on and calendar module. It is up to you to make use of all the available options for customizing Community Server so that you can effectively reap the rich benefits of this application.

# 9

# Working with Settings

In the previous chapter, you learned how to modify the look and feel of your site in various ways. In this chapter, we will explore the important settings that are used for managing a Community Server site. You will also learn how to modify the contact information, date, time, and email-related settings. We will also examine how to control the activities of the users registered on the site by tracking their IP addresses.

## Overview

The **Settings** section inside the **Site Administration** page contains several options for managing content, applications, contact information, date, time, and much more. It is important for you as an administrator to understand the working of each and every setting so that you can employ them as and when required. You, as an administrator would ideally use most of these settings, hence should surely be familiar with all of them. Let us examine each one of the options included under the section in detail.

## Managing General Site Settings

In order to enable advanced functionalities such as ink, site URL, EULA graphic, and other related settings, you should click the **General Site Settings** link located under the **Settings** section. The changes made to these settings will affect the whole site globally. They are also known as site-wide settings. Let us examine each one of these settings in detail.

## Enable Ink

This option enables you to write posts using an ink-enabled writing surface, typically called a **whiteboard,** and is disabled by default. The whiteboard becomes a part of the text editor when this setting is enabled. The **Ink** feature is a new addition to

Community Server and is introduced mainly for the purpose of **Tablet PC** users. It will enable them to use either the Stylus pen or hand-to-post content.

 You should install the Tablet PC Software Development Kit (SDK) locally or on the remote server if you don't have a Tablet PC to take advantage of Ink functionality.

Moreover, users should activate the **Enable Ink** setting in the **Site Options** tab on their profile page, even though the administrator has enabled it globally on the **Dashboard**, in order to take advantage of this functionality.

# Display Site Description

If this is enabled, the site description will be displayed on the top of every page below the site title. This option is enabled by default.

# Display Current Time

If this is enabled, the current time will be displayed on the home page of the site. This option is enabled by default and will be localized as per the setting on the user profile. You should note that this is a legacy option from the original ASP forums starter kit and is currently not used in Community Server.

# Display Who is Online

If this is enabled, the **Who is Online** section will be displayed on the bottom of the forums home page as shown below:

| Who is Online |
|---|
| There are **0** guest(s) online. There are **2** of **6** member(s) online - admin, packt |

# Display Site Statistics

If this is enabled, the **Forum Statistics** section will be displayed on the bottom of the forum's homepage as shown next:

**Forum Statistics**

**6** users have contributed to **13** threads and **13** posts.

In the past 24 hours, we have **1** new thread(s), **1** new post(s), and **0** new user(s).

In the past 3 days, the most popular thread for everyone has been "Working with Checkboxes using...". The post with the most views is "Working with Checkboxes using...". The most replies were made to "Working with Checkboxes using...".

Please welcome our newest member **rob howard**.

# Enable Display Names

With the help of this option, the name as specified in the **About** tab on the profile page will be displayed all over the site instead of the real username as shown below. You should also note that these names need not be unique. This setting is disabled by default and will be available only if the relevant user has activated the **Enable Display Name** setting in the **Site Options** tab on their profile page.

 You can open the profile page by clicking the link associated with the username at the top of the home page.

# Default Site URL

This setting specifies the URL for accessing the home page of your site. By default, the value will be the one that you gave at the time of installation. For our sample site, the URL will be `http://localhost/cs21`. Typically, the URL will point to the root directory of the Community Server installation and you can access the site just by supplying its web address.

# Terms of Service

This setting enables you to specify a URL to activate the **Site Terms** option. It displays a checkbox along with a link to the site's Terms of Service agreement. Your users will have an opportunity to view and approve the agreement during the registration process.

## Enable Content Language Filters

This setting will enable users to filter content based on language filters defined within their profile.

## Display EULA Graphic

If this is enabled, the **End User License Agreement (EULA)** graphic will be displayed in the footer of all pages of your Community Server site. This setting is enabled by default.

# Managing Site Content

The options included on the **Site Name & Description** page enable you to manage content oriented towards the site such as name, description, meta tags, and copyright notices. Let us examine each of the settings in detail.

## Site Name

You can specify a title for your site with the help of this setting. Actually, once you log in as an administrator, you can click on the title portion at the top of the site and enter the required name for your site. This feature is available from Community Server 2.0 and above, and it is the recommended method of changing the site name.

## Site Description

You can specify a description for your site using this setting. Actually, once you log in as an administrator, you can click on the description portion below the site title and enter the required information. This feature is available from Community Server 2.0 and above and it is the recommended method of providing a description for your site.

## Search Meta Description

You can specify a text, which will be used as a description for your site's Meta tag. Search engines will use this information to locate and process your site on the World Wide Web. Community Server will automatically populate the entered description on all pages of the site.

## Search Meta Keywords

You can specify keywords separated by commas, which will be used as keywords for your site's Meta tag. Search engines will use these keywords to locate and process your site on the World Wide Web. Community Server will automatically populate the entered keywords on all pages of the site.

# Raw Header

With the help of this setting, you can display additional content on the top (header) of the site. You can either enter content as plain text or as HTML tags on the field.

# Copyright Notice

With the help of this setting, you can enter the HTML tag with the relevant URL where the **copyright notice** for the site is located. The corresponding link and the URL will be added to the bottom of each page on your site. The format of the HTML tag should look as shown below:

```
<a href = "http://www.visualanand.net/csbook/copyright.
aspx">Copyright</a>
```

# Applications

You can enable or disable forums, blogs, photo galleries, file galleries, and reader and roller using the options on this page. These options will be useful if you want to use Community Server only for the purpose of one or two applications. For instance, if you would like to use the site only for the purpose of blog and forum then you can activate **Disable Forum** and **Disable Blogs** option and deactivate all other applications as shown below:

Your users will then be able to access only blogs and forums. In the same way, you can enable or disable applications according to your requirements.

# Managing Contact Information

You can specify contact-related information by clicking the **Contact Info** link from the **Settings** section. Community Server uses the specified information for messaging purposes.

## Admin Email Address

You should supply an email address for the site administrator on this field. Community Server uses the address specified here to send notifications and other related information to the site administrator.

## Company/Organization Name

You should supply a name for your company or organization. This information is required for the purpose of COPPA.

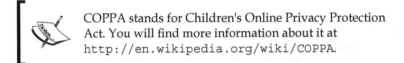

[ COPPA stands for Children's Online Privacy Protection Act. You will find more information about it at http://en.wikipedia.org/wiki/COPPA. ]

## Company/Organization Email Address

You should supply an email address for your company or organization.

## Company/Organization Fax Number

You should supply a fax number for your company or organization. Community Server uses this number to send faxes of COPPA forms as and when necessary.

## Company/Organization Address

You should supply the correct shipping address of your company or organization. Community Server uses this address to send copies of COPPA forms as and when necessary.

# Managing RSS Settings

RSS is the latest method of content delivery. With the help of the **RSS Settings** link, you can manage RSS-related settings associated with your site.

## Enable Secure Syndication

If this is enabled, Community Server will create a unique URL per feed to enable registered users to view feeds securely. These feeds are not accessible for anonymous users. This setting is enabled by default.

## Enable RSS Search

If this is enabled, users are allowed to create syndicated feeds that contain the results of a search. This setting is enabled by default.

# Managing Post Settings

With the help of the **Post Settings** link, you can manage and control settings that are relevant to posts. Let us examine each one of them in detail.

## Enable Anonymous Posting

If this is enabled, non-authenticated users are allowed to make posts and comments to the blogs and forums. This setting will override the default settings and permissions made under the specific section of each application. This setting is disabled by default.

## Enable Post Censorship

If this is enabled, posts are filtered for censored words. These words are listed in the **Manage/Create Censorships** page located under the **System Tools** section. Community Server will replace those words with the replacement criteria specified on the page.

We will examine more about censorship in Chapter 11.

## Allow Emoticons

If this is enabled, you can choose emoticons or smilies from a list whenever you compose a message. This setting is enabled by default but it will be available to you only if you manually enable it in the **Site Options** tab on the profile page. The emoticons list will appear on the text editor but the appearance will be different depending upon the kind of editor you have selected to use.

# Forum Rating Type

This setting specifies a rating type for the forum. It controls whether rating occurs at the thread level or for each individual post. If **Thread Rating** is enabled then users can only submit rating at the thread level. This means that they can post their rating on the first post of the thread. On the other hand if **Post Rating** is enabled then users can submit ratings on individual posts.

# User Posting Performance

This setting specifies how active an user is within the forum. If **Post Count** is enabled then each post made by the specific user is counted and displayed along with the post. On the other hand if user rank is enabled, then users are made active on the basis of their ranks.

# Display User Rank as a Picture

This setting denotes whether the user performance should be displayed as a pictured rank picture instead of text. By default it is displayed as a text.

# Search Results/Page

This setting specifies how many posts should be displayed on the search result page when a user performs a search on the site. The default setting is 10 but you can modify this to any value (up to 9999) depending upon the requirements of your site.

# Number of Top Posters

This setting specifies the number of top posters that should be displayed under the **Site Statistics** section at the bottom of the **Forums** home page. The corresponding usernames of those who have made top posts will be displayed. The default value is **10**. However, the maximum value is 100 and the minimum is one.

# Managing Date and Time Settings

You can specify date- and time-related settings that will be used by the Community Server for various purposes by selecting the **Date/Time Settings** link from the **Settings** section. Let us examine each of them in detail.

# Time Zone

As an administrator, you can specify a **Time zone** using the setting. However, your users can override this setting by selecting a **Time zone** in the **Site Options** tab on the profile. The drop-down box shows a list of zones and you need to pick an option from it depending upon the time zone in which the SQL server holding the Community Server database is located. Community Server uses this setting to display time-related information on the site.

# Date Format

You can specify a format for the display of dates using this setting. The drop-down box shows a list of date formats as shown in the screenshot below and you need to pick an option from it depending upon your preferences; but you should note that the users can override this setting in their profile. Community Server uses this setting to format the display of date-related information on the blogs and forums for anonymous users. The default format is **Day, Month Days Year.**

# Time Format

You can specify a format for the display of time on the site using this setting. The drop-down box shows a list of time formats as shown in the following screenshot, and you need to pick an option from it depending upon your preferences; but you should note that the users can override this setting in their profile. Community Server uses this setting to display time-related information on the blogs and forums. The default format is **12 hour single digit**.

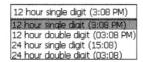

Any changes made here are immediately reflected on the site.

# Thread Date Filter

You can specify criteria for filtering threads using this setting. The default option is **Newer than 2 Months,** but you can pick your choice from a list as shown in the screenshot below. This means that all those threads that were posted during the last two months are displayed when a user performs a search query on the forum.

If **Show All** is selected then all the threads are displayed on the search result page.

# Managing Email Settings

You can manage email-related settings such as SMTP Server, SMTP login name, and SMTP password by selecting the **Email Settings** link. Emails generated by Community Server can only be delivered only if these settings are correct. Let us examine each of these settings in detail.

# Enable Email

If disabled, the email system will not function. Hence any feature that generates an email such as Forgot Password, Post Moderation, and Notification to registered users will not work until you enable the setting.

# Email Encoding

This setting specifies the default email encoding that will be used with all email messages. The default value is **utf-8,** and it also determines the character set. Some of the other possible values are us-ASCII, utf-7 or unicode.

UTF-8 stands for 8-bit Unicode Transformation Format.
You will find more information at:
`http://en.wikipedia.org/wiki/Utf-8`

# Email Throttle

This setting specifies the maximum number of emails that can be sent at a time.
The default setting is **-1** and this means infinite. If you set the value to 10 then
Community Server will only deliver 10 emails at a time.

# SMTP Server

This setting denotes the name of your SMTP server. The default value is **localhost** for
local systems. You need to specify the correct SMTP server name as supplied by your
host or network administrator.

**SMTP** stands for **Simple Mail Transfer Protocol** and it is
through this protocol emails are delivered to the recipients
from the server.

# Use Windows Integrated Authentication

If this is enabled, Community Server uses Windows Integrated Authentication to log
in to the SMTP server. Typically this is only used in a Windows domain environment
where the application pool that Community Server is executing in is authenticating
under a domain account and the same account has rights to the SMTP server.

# SMTP Server Login Required

You need to enable this setting if your remote server requires you to give credentials
to the SMTP server to send emails. Normally, username and password are supplied.
If you are not sure about this setting then you need to contact either your hosting
service provider or Internet Service Provider (ISP) to seek clarification.

# SMTP Server Login Name

You need to specify the login name of your SMTP server in this field. Typically, it
will be your full email address in the format *username@domain.com*.

# SMTP Server Password

You need to specify the password of your SMTP server in this field. Typically, it will be the password of the email address that you supplied earlier.

# SMTP Port Number

You need to specify the port number of your SMTP server on this field. Normally, it will be 25. However, you should note that changing this value allows Community Server to use SMTP servers that have been configured to use a non standard port such as 26. Some hosting providers use 26 as SMTP port since many Internet Service Providers block the default port, which is 25.

# Tracking the IP Address

With the increase in cyber crime, you have to track the Internet Protocol (IP) addresses of the posters to your Community Server site, thereby protecting your website against hackers and those who post unwanted submissions. Community Server provides a robust tracking mechanism by which you can know the original IP address of the user. This allows administrators to report the IP address of any unwanted activity to a law authority and allows licensed Community Server sites to ban the IP address. This feature is mainly used in forums. In order to manage the IP Address Tracking mechanism, you need to click the **IP Address Tracking** link. Let us now examine the options in detail.

# Enable Tracking of Poster IP Address

If enabled, Community Server stores the IP address of each user who posts messages on the forum. The IP address is displayed on the bottom of each post on the forum as shown below:

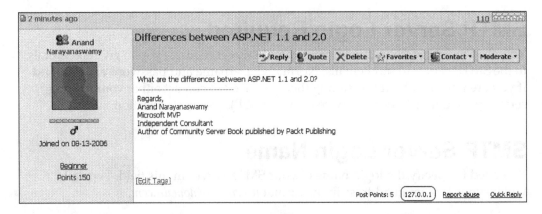

From the previous screenshot, you can infer that the post has been made from a local system with the default IP address 127.0.0.1 and not from a remote server.

 By default, the IP address is visible only for administrators.

## Display Poster IP Address Publicly

If this is enabled, the IP address is visible to all users and will be displayed along with all the posts on the site. This setting is disabled by default, because the public display of the posters' IP address may be considered as an invasion of privacy. Hence, in most situations this setting will not be enabled.

## Display Poster IP Address only to Administrators & Moderators

If this is enabled, the IP address of the poster will be visible only to the site Administrator and moderators. It will not be visible for an ordinary registered user. You should disable the previously discussed setting **Display Poster IP Address Publicly** in order to see the real working of this setting. If you enable that setting then the IP address will be displayed even if you are not an administrator or moderator.

## Summary

In this chapter, you have learned about the usage and management of the important aspects involved with posts, RSS, email, date, and time. Towards the end of this chapter, we have examined how to track the IP address of each poster, so that you can control the activities of your site in an effective manner.

The next chapter will examine the generation of various reports using Community Server.

# 10
# Working with Reports

We have so far examined the creation and management of various applications included with Community Server such as blogs, forums, galleries, reader, and roller and the different methods of customization. In this chapter, we will explore the usage of various kinds of reports included with Community Server. You will also learn about the creation of SQL jobs, required for generating various kinds of reports.

## Overview

Community Server includes a reporting functionality, which the Administrators can use to keep track of various activities on the site. You can generate and view various kinds of reports such as the exceptions report and the jobs report by clicking the relevant links located under the **Reports** navigation panel by selecting the **Administration** link on the **Dashboard**. Moreover, you can also generate reports pertaining to the various activities of the site, blogs, and forums by clicking the link titled **Reporting** from the dashboard. But this feature is only available in the standard (and above) versions of Community Server.

 You can purchase a license for Community Server from https://store.telligent.com/FamilyProducts.aspx?id=1. You will learn about the steps required for the installation of a license in Chapter 11.

You should also note that some of the functionalities will work only in a live server environment as they need to access the relevant SQL job at a specific time. Let us examine the working of each one of these reports in detail:

# Working with the Exceptions Report

In programming jargon, exceptions mean run-time errors. We often face a lot of problems when we run applications either locally or on a remote server. Community Server enables you to generate these kinds of errors in a report format sorted by the date of their occurrence. By default, a report of all exceptions is generated and displayed upon selecting the **Exceptions Report** link located under the **Reports** section from the **Site Administration** page as shown in the following screenshot:

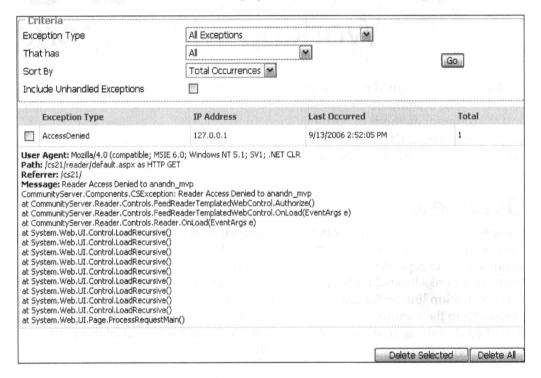

You can access the **Site Administration** page by clicking the **Control Panel** link and selecting the **Administration** link from the **Dashboard**.

As you can observe from the above screenshot, the report shows the type of exception, the IP address from where it occurred, the date of occurrence, and the number of times the specified error occurred. It also displays the browser and operating system used when the exception occurred, its path, and the sequence of events that led to the exception in detail.

You should note that the reports will look different when you generate them using Community Server.

You can either keep the reports or delete them from the system by clicking the **Delete Selected** button. You can also delete all the exceptions by clicking the **Delete All** button.

# Filtering the Exceptions Report

You can generate reports based on the type of exception by selecting the relevant exception from the **Exception Type** dropdown. You can also filter the report based on the frequency of occurrence by selecting the relevant option from the **That has** dropdown. The report will be blank if no exceptions have occurred, matching the criteria that you have selected.

# Working with the Jobs Report

Community Server runs certain jobs as services in the background, which are preconfigured by the application itself. You can view a detailed report of all jobs by selecting the **Jobs Report** link located under the **Reports** section from the **Site Administration** page as shown in the following screenshot:

## Jobs sharing a thread

| Type | Enabled | Is Running | Start | End | Success |
|---|---|---|---|---|---|
| CommunityServer.Galleries.Components.RebuildThumbnailsJob | True | False | 7/6/2006 3:53:30 PM | 7/6/2006 3:53:30 PM | 7/6/2006 3:53:30 PM |
| CommunityServer.Components.SiteStatisticsJob | True | False | 7/6/2006 3:53:30 PM | 7/6/2006 3:53:30 PM | 7/6/2006 3:53:30 PM |
| CommunityServer.Components.SearchBarrel.ForumsSearchJob | True | False | 7/6/2006 3:53:30 PM | 7/6/2006 3:53:30 PM | 7/6/2006 3:53:30 PM |
| CommunityServer.Components.EventLogJob | True | False | 7/6/2006 3:53:30 PM | 7/6/2006 3:53:30 PM | 7/6/2006 3:53:30 PM |
| CommunityServer.Components.SearchBarrel.GallerySearchJob | True | False | 7/6/2006 3:53:30 PM | 7/6/2006 3:53:30 PM | 7/6/2006 3:53:30 PM |
| CommunityServer.Components.ReferralsJob | True | False | 7/6/2006 3:53:30 PM | 7/6/2006 3:53:30 PM | 7/6/2006 3:53:30 PM |
| CommunityServer.Components.SearchBarrel.WeblogSearchJob | True | False | 7/6/2006 3:53:30 PM | 7/6/2006 3:53:30 PM | 7/6/2006 3:53:30 PM |
| CommunityServer.Components.PostAttachmentCleanupJob | True | False | 7/6/2006 3:53:30 PM | 7/6/2006 3:53:30 PM | 7/6/2006 3:53:30 PM |

As you can see from the screenshot on the previous page, the report shows the type of job, whether it is enabled, the current status, and the relevant start, end, and success date and time. All these jobs will run every one minute as specified in the **Interval** setting under the **Jobs Service Statistics** section. A frequency of 15 minute for the jobs interval should only be used for testing purposes; you should change it in the `communityserver.config` file for production systems.

Moreover, the report has been divided into two parts. While the first part displays those jobs that share a thread, the second part displays all the jobs that are running in their own thread as shown in the following screenshot:

### Jobs on their own thread

| Type | Enabled | Is Running | Start | End | Success |
|------|---------|------------|-------|-----|---------|
| CommunityServer.Components.EmailJob | True | False | 7/6/2006 4:12:17 PM | 7/6/2006 4:12:17 PM | 7/6/2006 4:12:17 PM |
| CommunityServer.Reader.Components.FeedUpdater | True | False | 7/6/2006 4:16:26 PM | 7/6/2006 4:16:27 PM | 7/6/2006 4:16:27 PM |

# Reporting with Community Server

With the release of Community Server 2.1, the activity reporting functionality has been separated and you can access it by clicking the **Reporting** link from the **Dashboard**. You will find three separate navigation panels titled **Site**, **Blogs**, and **Forums** on the left-hand side of the page. Each panel consists of several options with which you can access the relevant activity and other usage-related reports.

## Generating Reports for the Site

The **Site** panel contains three options for generating activity reports—**Page Views**, **User Activity**, and **Overview**. The **Page Views** report displays the URL of the visited pages along with the page views for each URL within the specified criteria. You can select the relevant start and end dates from the criteria panel as shown below:

Community Server displays a calendar upon clicking the icon shown beside each date.

You can either generate the report or export it as a **Microsoft Office Excel Comma Separated Values (CSV)** file format. You can do this for all reports.

The **User Activity** report generates a list of unique IP addresses that have visited the site along with the page views for that visitor within the specified criteria. The interface looks similar to that of the generation of the page views report.

 You should create an SQL job using SQL Server 2005 that executes the *cs_UserActivityNightlyJob* stored procedure in order to generate the user activity report. Refer to the section *Creating SQL Jobs* for more information regarding the creation of the SQL job.

The **Overview** report lists the total number of registered users, threads, and posts within the specified criteria as shown below:

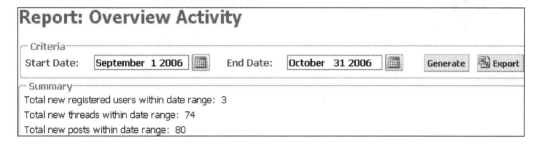

## Generating Reports for Blogs

You can generate blog activity report by selecting the **Blog Activity** link located under the **Blogs** panel in the **Dashboard**. The report includes a listing of all blogs on the site in a grid and will also shows the total blogs, total enabled blogs, total disabled blogs, and the total number of blogs active between the search dates. You can filter the report with a specific start and end date and the report will be generated based upon the selected criteria.

 You should create an SQL job using SQL Server 2005 that executes the *cs_BlogActivityNightlyJob* stored procedure in order to generate the blog activity report. Refer to the section *Creating SQL Jobs* for more information regarding the creation of the SQL job.

In addition to the **Blog Activity** report, you can also generate reports for popular blog topics with reference to **Views** and **Comments**. The **Popular Topics by Views** link enables you to generate a list of the top 25 blog posts based on the number of hits or views each received since its creation date with reference to the specified start and end dates as shown in the following screenshot:

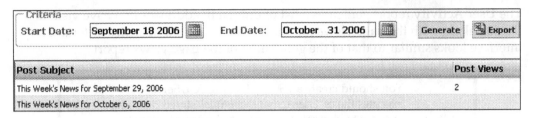

In the same way, the **Popular Topics by Comments** link enables you to generate a list of the top 25 blog posts based on the number of comments that have been posted since the creation of each post with reference to the specified start and end dates.

# Generating Reports for Forums

You can generate a forum activity report by selecting the **Forum Post Activity** link located under the **Forums** panel inside the **Reporting** link. The report specifies the total number of active forums within the specified date range in addition to forum name, number of new replies, number of new threads, and active users as shown below:

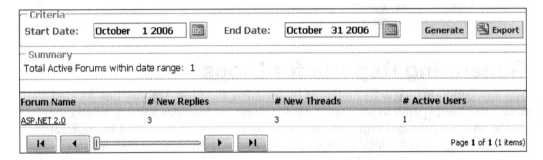

As you can see there is only one forum that was active between the specified start and end date. You can navigate directly to the relevant forum if you click on the link in the **Forum Name** column.

In addition to the **Forum Activity** report, you can also generate reports for popular forum topics with reference to **Views** and **Replies**. The **Popular Topics by Views** link enables you to generate a list of the top 25 forum posts based on the number of hits or views each received, since its creation date, with reference to the specified start and end dates as shown next:

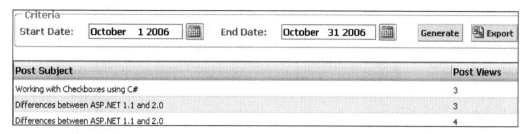

| Post Subject | Post Views |
|---|---|
| Working with Checkboxes using C# | 3 |
| Differences between ASP.NET 1.1 and 2.0 | 3 |
| Differences between ASP.NET 1.1 and 2.0 | 4 |

Similarly, the **Popular Topics by Replies** link enables you to generate a list of the top 25 blog posts based on the number of replies since their creation, with reference to the specified start and end dates.

The activity reports are not generated by default. You have to perform certain additional tasks as outlined in the section *Setting up Activity Reports* in order for the Community Server to generate reports.

# Working with SQL Jobs

As noted earlier, you should create the relevant SQL jobs using SQL Server 2005 Management Studio before beginning to generate user and blog activity reports. This can be done by logging into SQL Server 2005 and starting the SQL Server Agent service (by default, this service is stopped). You can start the service by right-clicking SQL Server Agent and selecting **Start** from the pop-up menu as shown in the screenshot below:

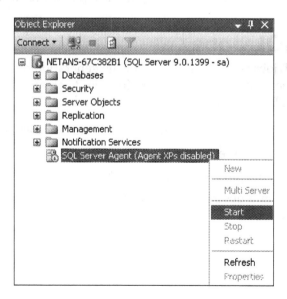

In order to create SQL jobs you need to install SQL Server 2005 Developer Edition. You can download a trial version of it from `http://www.microsoft.com/sql/downloads/trial-software.mspx`

SQL Server 2005 will display a progress indicator during the starting of the service. Once the service has been started follow the steps outlined below to set up activity reports:

1. Add the following code to the `<httpModules>` section of the `web.config` file:

```
<add name="CSVisitors" type="CommunityServer.
        VisitorCountHttpModule, CommunityServer.Components" />
```

2. Add the following code to the `<jobs>` section of the `CommunityServer.config` file. This file can be located inside the root directory of Community Server installation.

```
<job name = "Visitors" type = "CommunityServer.Components.
        VisitorsJob, CommunityServer.Components" enabled =
        "true" enableShutDown = "false" />
```

3. Create an SQL job using SQL Server 2005 that runs every morning at 1:30 AM or anytime after midnight that executes the *cs_UserActivityNightlyJob* stored procedure.

4. Create the relevant SQL job that runs every morning at 1:00 AM or anytime after midnight that executes the *cs_BlogActivityNightlyJob* stored procedure.

# Creating SQL Jobs

The creation of SQL jobs is a critical aspect for the generation of reports, as reports are created and generated based on the jobs. In order to create an SQL job, you should follow the following steps:

1. Log in to the SQL Server 2005 management studio as an administrator.

2. Expand the SQL Server Agent tree.

3. Right-click on the **jobs** section and select **New Job**.

4. Enter a name and description for the job as shown in the following screenshot:

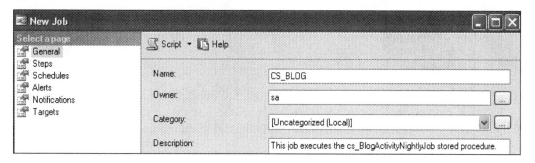

5. Check-mark the **Enabled** option so that the job will run immediately following its creation.

6. From the **Job Properties** dialog, navigate to the **Steps** page.

>  In order to open **Job Properties** dialog, right click the created job name from the **Jobs** tree and select **Properties** from the pop-up menu.

7. Select the **New** button and enter the required information as shown in the screenshot below. You need to select the name of your database from the dropdown.

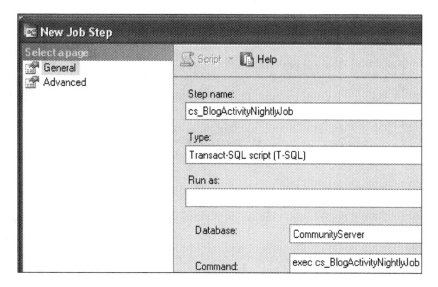

8. The above job step will execute a stored procedure. The **Parse** button located at the bottom of the **New Job Step** dialog enables you to check the syntax of your SQL command. Click the **OK** button to return to the **Job Properties** dialog.

9. Your next activity is to set a schedule for the above job step.

10. For this purpose, select **Schedules** from the left side navigation bar. Select the **New** button and set the desired schedule by giving a name and its frequency as shown in the screenshot below:

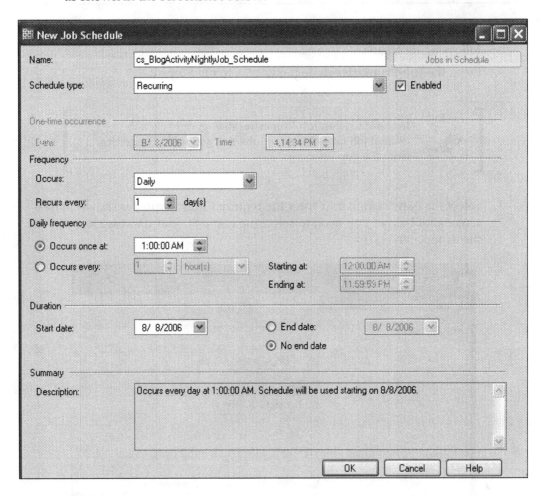

11. The above schedule signifies that the stored procedure will run every day at 1.00 AM starting from August 8, 2006. Click the **OK** button to return to the **Job Properties** page.

12. With the above step, the process of creation of an SQL job has been completed. Click the **OK** button to return to the SQL Server 2005 Management Studio.

Similarly, you should create a job for the *cs_UserActivityNightlyJob* stored procedure. The SQL job will not run if you turn off your system. This is not applicable for a remote hosting server, which will always be on.

> You need to contact your hosting service provider to create the required SQL jobs for your site if you don't have access to the remote hosting server.

# Summary

Reporting is one of the critical activities in every application. This holds true for Community Server as well. With the help of the reporting functionality, site administrators can generate and view different kinds of reports. In addition to the exceptions and jobs reports, we have also examined the working of user, blog and forum activity reports. We also examined the creation of the SQL jobs that require to be created in a live hosting environment for generating various activity reports.

# 11
# Working with System Tools

As an Administrator of Community Server, you need to properly manage critical functions such as those of advertisements, licenses, and articles. Moreover, you will be required to restrict the usage of site by implementing spam control measures included with Community Server. In this chapter, you will learn how to manage all of these functions in detail.

## Getting Started

Once you are logged in to the site as an Administrator, click the **Control Panel** link from the top navigation bar. Click **Administration** and expand the **System Tools** panel. You will see a list of options as shown the following screenshot:

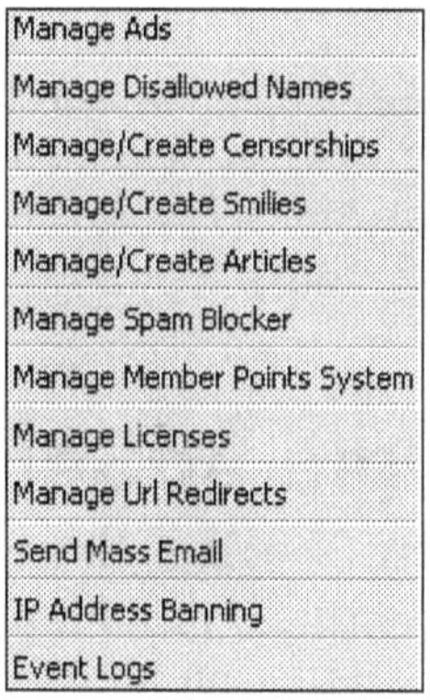

| |
|---|
| Manage Ads |
| Manage Disallowed Names |
| Manage/Create Censorships |
| Manage/Create Smilies |
| Manage/Create Articles |
| Manage Spam Blocker |
| Manage Member Points System |
| Manage Licenses |
| Manage Url Redirects |
| Send Mass Email |
| IP Address Banning |
| Event Logs |

Let us now examine the options available in the **System Tool** panel in detail.

# Working with Ads

Nowadays, advertisements forms a part and parcel of each and every website. The Administrator of the site will earn revenue as and when users click on the displayed advertisements. The ads can either be text or images. You can implement various kinds of popular advertisement systems such as Google AdSense or Amazon's affiliate system on your Community Server site depending upon the requirements.

As an Administrator, you can enable advertisements from **Dashboard | Administration** by selecting the **Manage Ads** link located under **System Tools**. Let us examine each of the options available for the management of ads in detail.

## Enabling Ads

As soon as you activate the **Enable Ads** option from the **Manage Ads** page, a link titled **Ad PlaceHolder** will be added to the top and bottom portion of the home page.

An important feature of this setting is that the relevant ad will be displayed on each page of the site.

An Administrator can easily add the required code for the display of ads by double-clicking the **Ad PlaceHolder** link.

In order to manually configure ads for your site, you need to modify Skin-Ads.ascx located under the \Themes\ default\Skins directory inside the root of your Community Server site.

## Implementing Google AdSense on your site

Let us now examine how to display Google AdSense on the site. As mentioned above, you can add the code for the display of ads either at the top or bottom of the page by double-clicking the relevant placeholders.

You can generate the code for Adsense for content, AdSense for search, and referrals by logging in at `http://www.google.com/adsense` if you are already a member of Google's AdSense Program. Otherwise, you should apply and wait for the approval email from Google.

As soon as you double-click an **Ad PlaceHolder** link, a pop-up dialog box will be displayed. You have to add the required code as shown below:

```
<center>
<script type="text/javascript"><!--
google_ad_client = "pub-XXXXXXXXXXXXXXXXXXXXX";
google_ad_width = 468;
google_ad_height = 60;
google_ad_format = "468x60_as";
google_ad_type = "text";
google_ad_channel ="";
//--></script>
<script type="text/javascript"
  src="http://pagead2.googlesyndication.com/pagead/show_ads.js">
</script>
</center>
```

As you can see from the above code, we have deliberately masked the value of `google_ad_client` property for security reasons. Your daily earnings are calculated with reference to this property and it is extremely important to supply the correct code, which you generated and copied by logging into the website of Google AdSense. The relevant ad will be displayed on the home page of the site immediately on clicking the **Save Changes** button, as shown below:

| Enhanced Network Gateway | Bit Level Replication | DNS Expert Professional |
|---|---|---|
| Cost Effective Videoconferencing Between IP And ISDN Networks. | Any OS Any Network Fast Bit Level Copy Free Trial | Comprehensive analyzing software. Detailed report on your DNS health. |
| LifeSize.com | www.filereplicationpro.com | www.menandmice.com |

Ads by Google                                                    Advertise on this site

# Implementing Amazon Associates on your Site

Like Google's AdSense program, Amazon also provides an Associates or Affiliate scheme for its customers. You can either display a text link or an image on your site and revenues are generated based on each sale made through the site. The commissions are calculated based upon the link and each customer will have to add a different Associate code for earning income. The relevant Associate code will be embedded inside the HTML code. In this section, we will examine how to display an advertisement using Amazon's Associates Program on your site.

 You need to register at `http://associates.amazon.com/gp/associates/join/102-0670951-7143347` in order to generate the required code for the purpose of displaying advertisements.

In order to display a particular advertisement, you first have to generate the HTML code from the **Build Links** page by logging into your affiliate section located at `http://associates.amazon.com`. You will then need to double-click the **Ad PlaceHolder** link from the home page of your Community Server site and add the required code, which you copied from the website of Amazon.

The relevant advertisement will be displayed as shown below, on the home page of the site, immediately upon clicking the **Save Changes** button.

# Implementing Inline Ads

The **Enable Inline Ad Control** option inside the **Manage Ads** page enables you to showcase skinned advertisements. The ads have to be configured and sourced from third party advertisement software such as BanManPro (`http://www.banmanpro.com`). You have to place the necessary JavaScript to display ads, which you generated by using the ad serving software, by double-clicking the **Ad via Inline Control** link from the home page of your Community Server site.

# Working with Disallowed Names

With the help of the **Manage Disallowed Names** setting, the Administrator can prevent inappropriate names, called disallowed names, from being displayed on the site and being used as usernames during user registration. Community Server provides a list of some of these disallowed names, which are displayed in the page that appears after clicking the **Manage Disallowed Names** setting. You can also create them by supplying the name to be disallowed in the **Name** field and clicking the **Create** button as shown below:

From the above screenshot you can see that a disallowed name **moderator** is created that will be added in the list of disallowed names. Hence the Community Server will prohibit any user registering as **moderator** and display a message: **Filled in username is prohibited on this forum. Please choose other username**.

Now you know how to disallow a user from registering as **moderator**, you can also disallow names that are similar to this username like moderator1, moderatoradmin, and so on.

You have to move to the page where all the disallowed names are displayed and scroll down to the name **moderator**. Click the **Edit** button, append an asterisk (*) to the name, and save the changes by clicking the **Update** button as shown in the screenshot below:

The modified name is added to the list of disallowed names and Community Server will prohibit any user registering with a username starting with **moderator**.

You should note that enclosing the word in asterisks as shown above will ban any name containing the string **mod**. As soon as you click the **Create** button, the name will be added to the disallowed names list as shown in the following screenshot:

You can also modify and delete the name by selecting the **Edit** and **Delete** buttons respectively from the **Actions** column. When a new member tries to register on the site and attempts to use the disallowed name a message is displayed on the registration page as shown in the screenshot overleaf:

**Sign in name, email, and password (required)**

Sign in Name: moderator     *

Choose Password:

Re-enter Password:

Email Address: communityserverbook@gmail.com    (your email address is not published)

Re-enter Email Address: communityserverbook@gmail.com

Timezone: (GMT -08:00) Pacific Time (US & Canada)

• Filled in username is prohibited on this forum. Please choose other username.

If an existing member attempts to change their display name by clicking the username link on the top of the site to a name that is in the disallowed name list, then Community Server will not accept the change. Community Server recognizes that the name is disallowed and will automatically display the permitted original username.

 You should note that disallowed names do not censor content in posts or comments.

# Working with Censorship

With the help of censorship, you can prevent unsuitable words or phrases from visitor-submitted content being displayed on your site. Community Server provides a list of obscene words with which it scans text. You can view them by clicking the **Manage/Create Censorships** setting.

A word that is found to be inappropriate will be replaced by text called a **Replacement Token**. By default, these tokens will be displayed in the form of three asterisks (***). However, you can edit them by selecting the **Edit** button and entering a new token as shown below:

abcd     ???                             **Update** | **Cancel**

Community Server will display the modified token for the corresponding word immediately after you select the **Update** button as shown in the screenshot.

abcd            ???                               **Edit** | **Delete**

# Creating Censored Words

Community Server provides an option to add a new word in the list of inappropriate words. In order to create a censored word, scroll down, and enter the desired word and a replacement token in the relevant field as below:

The relevant word will be added to the grid on clicking the **Create** button as shown below:

We have successfully created a word **pqrs** with a token ### corresponding to it. Let us now submit a post on the forum with the above created censored word. The final output will appear as below:

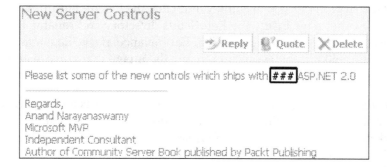

# Working with Smilies

Emoticons or Smilies are a smart way to express your behavior or attitude that can be conveyed along with your posts. You can manage them by selecting the **Manage/Create Smilies** setting. By default, Community Server provides an exhaustive collection of smilies as shown overleaf.

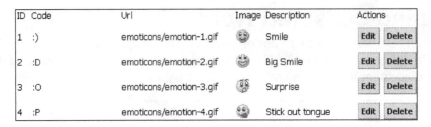

You can modify the **Code**, **URL**, **Image**, and **Description** of a particular smiley or emoticon by selecting the **Edit** button as shown below:

 By default, the images are stored in the **Emoticons** folder located inside the Community Server installation directory.

In order to add a smiley, scroll down to the bottom of the page, enter the **Code**, **URL**, and **Description** of the new smiley and click the **Create** button. You should upload the relevant image inside the **Emoticons** directory and rename the image according to the last item found on the list. For instance, if the file name of the last smiley is **emotion-60.gif**, then you can rename the image that you are going to add as **emotion-61.gif**.

Let us now discuss how to use emoticons. Log in to the site as a user and create a new post by selecting the **Write a New Post** button from the relevant forum. You need to pick an emoticon by clicking the **Insert Smiley** icon from the toolbar of the content editor and the corresponding emoticon will be displayed inside a pop-up window. The relevant code for the selected emoticon will be displayed in the editor as shown overleaf:

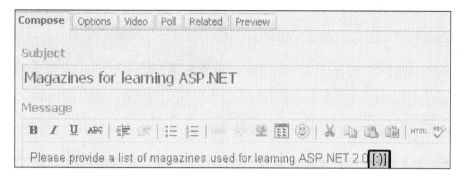

You should note from the above screenshot that the editor displays the code for the selected smiley. The associated image will be displayed when the post is submitted as shown in the following screenshot:

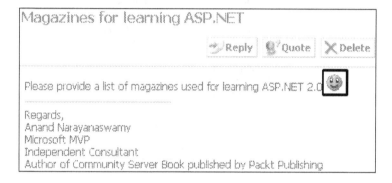

# Working with Articles

Articles are short content, compositions or publications on a certain subject posted on the site. You can link them while creating blog or forum posts. The difference between blog posts and articles is that your users can only view the posted content. They cannot post comments or rate the article. This feature will be useful if you would like to showcase certain content that doesn't require user feedback.

You can create and manage articles by clicking the **Manage/Create Articles** link. Community Server will display the content editor immediately after selecting the **Create new article** button from the **Manage Articles** page. The look and feel of the content editor will be the same as we saw while discussing blogs and forums.

You need to give the name for the article, a headline title, and the required content inside the content editor as shown in the following screenshot:

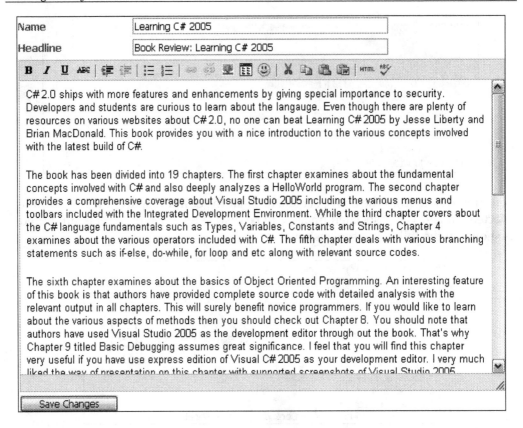

The above article is saved and created immediately upon clicking the **Save Changes** button. You can also immediately view the output after its creation as shown in the screenshot below:

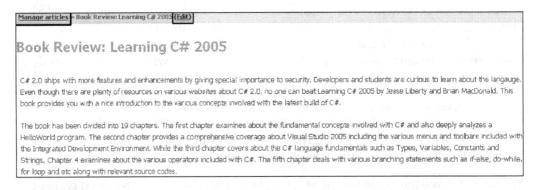

You can directly update the content of the article by selecting the **Edit** link and manage all the articles by clicking the **Manage** articles link at the top of the preview page of the article.

| Last Modified | Article Name | Actions | |
|---|---|---|---|
| 10/19/2006 3:25:16 PM | LearningC2005 | View | Edit |

You can not only view the articles but can also modify them by clicking the **Edit** button, which will display the content editor page populated with the relevant article. You need to click on the **Save Changes** button after updating the content. You can also delete the article by selecting the **\*Delete Immediately\*** button if you feel that the article is no longer required.

As you can see from the screenshot, Community Server uses part of the supplied name to create the file name. For our sample article opposite, the Uniform Resource Locator (URL) will be `http://localhost/cs21/content/LearningC2005.aspx`. You will notice that the spaces and hash that we gave in the **Name** field are automatically removed from the **Article Name** column.

# Working with Spam Blocker

Community Server provides an interface for blocking spam. Spam is often referred to as unsolicited and illegal posts and is used in conjunction with emails. The same policy also applies to forums as well. Popular forums may at some point attract spam, which detracts from genuine content posted. As an Administrator, you need to develop a mechanism to prevent these sorts of problems.

Community Server includes a built-in functionality with which site administrators can effectively manage spam. It can be accessed by clicking the **Manage Spam Blocker** link.

The Spam Blocker not only checks the forum posts but also the comments posted under each blog and photo galleries.

The Spam blocker interface displays an interface with two important options: **Site settings for marking comments as moderated** and **Site settings for deleting comments suspected as spam**. These settings work in relation to the rules specified under the **Rules** section. Let us examine these settings in detail.

The **Site settings for marking comments as moderated** option specifies the score value for moderating comments posted to the site. If a post generates a value equal to or above a particular limit set but below the value of the **Site settings for deleting comments suspected as spam option**, then that post is subject to moderation automatically. Community Server checks for the limits from the enabled rules. The default value is 5 and this means that any post that crosses this limit will be passed on to the moderator prior to display on the site. Any post that is below the value of 5 will be automatically visible on the site depending upon the site settings enabled by the Administrator.

The **Site settings for deleting comments suspected as spam** option will also work as discussed above with the difference that any post which crosses the value specified on the field will not appear on the site. Instead it will be available inside the **Deleted Posts** forum for further review. The default value for this setting is 10. However, site Administrators can change the value depending upon the requirement.

The Deleted Posts forum can be accessed only by a site administrator.

# Examining the Rules

Community Server includes a set of four rules **Bad Word Count, Forbidden Word, IP Count,** and **Link Count** as shown in the screenshot below:

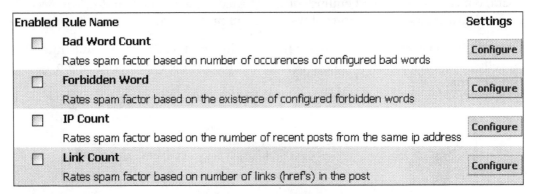

| Enabled | Rule Name | Settings |
|---------|-----------|----------|
| ☐ | **Bad Word Count**<br>Rates spam factor based on number of occurences of configured bad words | Configure |
| ☐ | **Forbidden Word**<br>Rates spam factor based on the existence of configured forbidden words | Configure |
| ☐ | **IP Count**<br>Rates spam factor based on the number of recent posts from the same ip address | Configure |
| ☐ | **Link Count**<br>Rates spam factor based on number of links (href's) in the post | Configure |

These rules effectively manage all spam-related content on the site. You can configure each rule by clicking the **Configure** button and activate the rule by selecting the **Enabled** checkbox from each row. Let us examine each one of the above rules in detail.

# Bad Word Count

This rule provides a list of bad words, which are used for filtering the content posted on the site. The site administrator can assign points for each bad word, specify how many times a bad word can appear in the post, and can also add new words as shown in the screenshot below:

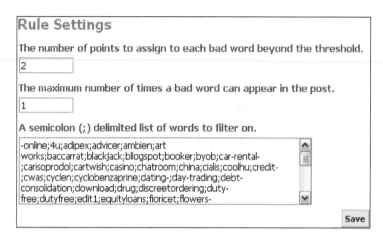

Community Server automatically filters the post when a specific bad word appears more than the specified maximum number of times. However, you can modify the setting according to your preferences.

 Rules are not enabled by default. The site administrator should enable them after going through their configuration.

# Forbidden Word

This setting specifies a list of forbidden or prohibited words. These words need not be bad. Community Server doesn't provide a list of these words like **Bad Words**. Instead administrators should provide them as shown below along with the number of points for each time in appears in a post. The default value for this rule is 5.

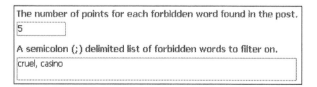

There is a marginal difference between a Bad Word and a Forbidden word.

The Bad Word Spam rule assigns points when a word considered bad appears more than once. For example, "casino" may be used in the context of a message so one appearance may be acceptable. However, multiple appearances of the same word will cause an accumulation of points towards being Spam. This rule has a threshold.

The Forbidden Word Spam rule assigns points whenever a word exists. Points are given for each instance of the word. This rule does not have a threshold.

# IP Count

With Community Server, you can manage posts based on IP addresses. The system will perform a check based on the number of recent posts from the same IP address. This is done to avoid malicious attempts to flood a forum with useless posts by a particular IP address. It consists of several settings as shown in the screenshot below:

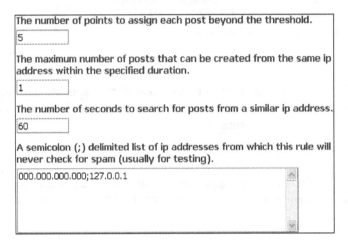

You can enter the number of points to assign each post beyond the threshold; the default value is 5. You need to specify the maximum number of posts that can be created from the same IP address within the specified period; the default value is 1. You also need to specify the time span to search for posts from the same IP address; the default value is 60 seconds. You may know certain IP addresses that do not require application of this rule. You can specify a list of these IP addresses separated by semicolons from which this rule will never check for spam.

# Link Count

The **Link Count** rule enables you to block any post that contains more than a specified number of links and is applicable only for blog comments. This rule has direct relationship with the **Site settings for marking comments as moderated** setting that is displayed on the **Manage Spam Blocker** page.

The number of points to assign each link beyond the threshold

2

The maximum number of links that can appear in the post.

0

Assuming the values of all the settings are set to default, users can post only 2 links along with their comments on each blog post. The remaining comments with more than 2 links will be visible only after the approval of the Administrator or moderator. Hence, if a user posts a comment with 3 links then the corresponding post will fetch 6 points (3 links * 2) and will be visible on the comments page after its approval by the Administrator. We have discussed about the approval of comments in Chapter 3 - *Working with Blogs*.

However, if you set the value of the **The maximum number of links that can appear in the post** setting to 1 then a maximum of 3 links will be displayed on the comments page. These link submissions don't require any moderation. However, the blog post will not display any comments which contain more than 3 links. This will be visible on the comments page as and when they are approved by the Administrator or moderator.

# Installing New Spam Rules

Telligent or other developers may develop enhanced spam content filtering controls and they will be available from the **Downloads** section of the official website as and when they are released. You have to copy the Dynamic Link Library (DLL) file of the downloaded new control and place it in the **bin** directory of your Community Server installation. Now you need to click the **Reload Rules** button located at the bottom of the **Manage Spam Blocker** page to enable the newly set rules in the Community Server.

# Working with the Member Points System

Community Server includes a system called **Member Points** with which you can allocate specified numbers of points according to the activities performed by each member on the site. These activities include submission of posts, posting a reply, and much more. But in order to work with this feature, you require a standard license or above of Community Server.

As an Administrator, you can manage points by clicking the **Manage Member Points System** setting. Firstly, you need to activate the **Enable Member Points System** setting from the **General** tab of the **Manage Member Points System** page. Let us examine the settings included in each tab in detail.

# General

With the help of the settings on this tab you can enable and control the visibility of points for posts and users.

## Enable the Member Points System

You can enable or disable member points by selecting the required value. By default, this setting is disabled. As noted earlier, you need to enable the setting. If it is enabled, points are calculated for both posts and users.

## Post Points Visibility

With the help of this setting, you can control the visibility of points measured for posts. By default, the points will be visible to all users of the site. But you can restrict the viewing of points by selecting the **Don't show to anyone** or **Show only to Administrators and Moderators** option from the drop-down box associated with the **Post Points Visibility** setting.

## User Points Visibility

With the help of this setting, you can control the visibility of points measured for users. By default, the points will be visible to all users of the site. But you can restrict the viewing of points by selecting the **Don't show to anyone** or **Show only to Administrators and Moderators** option from the drop-down box associated with the **User Points Visibility** setting.

# Factor Values

With the help of the settings on this tab you can specify the values with which the points will be calculated and displayed on the site.

# Post Factor

This setting specifies the amount for each post. The default value is 5; hence if a user submits 10 posts then that particular user will earn 50 points.

# Reply Factor

This setting specifies the amount for each reply made for the original post by users. The default value is 15 and if a user makes 2 replies then the original user who posted the download will get 30 points.

# Replier Factor

This setting specifies the amount for each unique reply made for the original post by users. The points will be counted only if a fresh user replies to a specific post. If a same user submits more than one reply then that will not be counted. The default value is 5.

# Rating Factor

This setting measures the amount of points each original poster will earn when somebody rates their posts on the site. The default value is 6.

# Download Factor

This setting specifies the amount for each download made from the original post by users. The default value is 5 and if a user downloads 2 files then the original user who posted the download will get 10 points.

# Downloader Factor

This setting specifies the amount for each unique download made from the original post by the users. The points will not be counted if the same user downloads the file more than once. The default value is 5.

# Favorite Post Factor

This setting signifies the amount of points which will accumulate when a user rates a particular post as favorite. The default value is 5.

# Favorite User Factor

This setting signifies the amount of points which will accumulate when a user rates a particular user as favourite. The default value is 100.

# Rater Factor

The points system not only benefits a user but also benefits those who rate a post or user. This setting signifies the amount of points that can be earned by a registered user when that user rates a post or user on the site.

# Calculate

This tab consists of a single button captioned **Calculate** and you should click it if you have made any modifications to the values for the various settings as mentioned previously.

Make sure to click the **Save** button after modifying the values before attempting to click the **Calculate** button.

# Viewing Member Points

The Member Points functionality is mainly implemented for forums. You can view the points earned by each user while accessing each post as shown in the following screenshot:

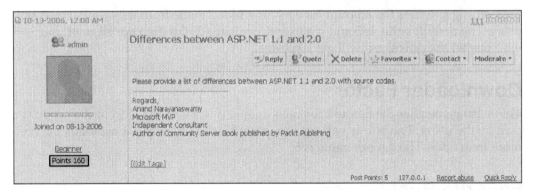

# Working with Licenses

As discussed in Chapter 1, the Express edition is available free of cost. To access extra functionality and resilience you may wish to consider the purchase of a license. As we explained in the chapter, there are different types of licenses and you need to purchase a license depending upon the requirements of your site.

The **System Tools** section provides a separate area for the installation and management of various licenses and it can be accessed by clicking the **Manage Licenses** link. In order to install a license, you need the required set of files, which will be emailed to you by Telligent as soon as you purchase a license for your site. It includes an XML file with the required information pertaining to the license and also a license agreement file in PDF format.

There is no need to request an additional license if you have installed Community Server 2.0 as the same license file can be used for Community Server 2.1.

You need to install the XML file in order to activate the license for your site by clicking the **Install** button after browsing and locating the required XML file. The path will be displayed inside the **Install License File** field. Community Server will display the required information regarding the installed license after the successful completion of the installation process as shown in the following screenshot:

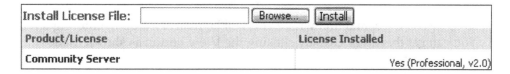

As you can observe from the above screenshot, a **Professional** edition license has been installed with the version number **2.0**. You can also purchase additional modules and install them using the **Manage Licenses** page.

With Community Server 2.0, license-related information is stored in the database rather than the file system as was done in the previous versions.

# Working with URL Redirects

Sometimes, you will be required to create special URLs for certain content that changes very frequently. In such cases you can employ a mechanism of uploading the content to one location and maintaining another link with which users can access that particular content. The advantage of this system is that you only need to perform modifications in one place. The users will access it using a special URL even if the original content changes very often. This concept is termed **URL Redirection**.

With Community Server, you can create URL Redirects very easily. Let us examine this functionality in detail.

You have to click the **Manage Url Redirects** link available under the **System Tools** section. You need to enter the URL where the original content has been uploaded in the **Redirect Url** field and also a short description about the URL in the **Description** field as shown below:

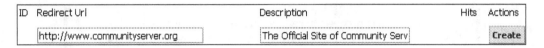

| ID | Redirect Url | Description | Hits | Actions |
|----|-------------|-------------|------|---------|
|    | http://www.communityserver.org | The Official Site of Community Serv | | Create |

Click the **Create** button to create the appropriate URL redirection link after entering the required information. The relevant Redirection URL will be created immediately as shown in the following screenshot:

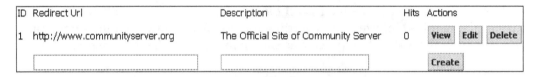

| ID | Redirect Url | Description | Hits | Actions |
|----|-------------|-------------|------|---------|
| 1 | http://www.communityserver.org | The Official Site of Community Server | 0 | View Edit Delete |
|    | | | | Create |

The above URL is the actual link where you will be redirected upon entering another URL. You can get this other URL by clicking the **View** button as shown in the following screenshot:

Copy/Paste the following url into any webpage:

http://localhost/cs21/r.ashx?1

Users of this url will be redirected to: http://www.communityserver.org

So far, **0** people have clicked on this url!

If you navigate to `http://localhost/cs21/r.ashx?1`, then you will be automatically redirected to `http://www.communityserver.org`. Hence, even if the content has been updated at `http://www.communityserver.org`, it will have no effect on the redirection URL as it always stays constant.

In addition to the URL the **Url Redirect** pop-up window showed above also displays the link statistics which shows how many users have so far accessed the redirection URL.

# Handling Mass Emails

Occasionally, you may wish to send general purpose emails to your members. The content of these emails can be related to maintenance issues, monthly newsletters, or any updates to the products you sell. As your site grows, the number of members who register on the site also increases. Hence, it will be cumbersome to send separate emails to all members.

Community Server includes a module for handling bulk emails and it can be accessed by clicking the **Send Mass Email** link. You will see a page that enables you to select a group to distribute the email to, from the **Recipient(s)** drop-down box, and compose the required content by supplying the required **Subject** and **Message** appropriately. You can take advantage of the rich features of the content editor as well.

Click the **Send** button to deliver the message to the concerned recipients after entering the required information.

# Banning an IP Address

Sometimes, your site may be either hacked or subjected to **Denial-of-Service** attacks. Immediately, you should try to stop these types of attacks in future. A nice way to do this is to find out the IP address of the attacker and then block that address using the various tools on the server. In most cases, you will not have access to these tools. In such a situation you have to find out alternative ways to resolve the problem.

Community Server includes a built-in functionality to ban an IP address and it can be accessed by clicking the **IP Address Banning** link. You should note that this functionality is available only if you have installed the standard version or above of Community Server.

You need to enter the required IP address and click on the **Add IP Address** button. You can also enter range such as **111.111.11.***. As soon as you click the button the IP address will be displayed on the screen as shown in the screenshot:

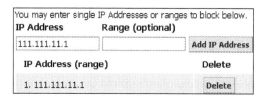

Once an IP Address has been blocked it can be deleted or unblocked by clicking the **Delete** button. You can also manually view the banned IP addresses from the **cs_BannedAddresses** table using the various tools for accessing databases such as SQL Server 2005 Express Edition or SQL Server 2005.

# Working with Event Log Viewer

Once Community Server has been successfully deployed, Administrators and users perform various activities. These activities are recorded in the **Event Log Viewer** page, as shown in the screenshot overleaf, which can be accessed by clicking the **Event Logs** link. The page includes starting and stopping of various services included with Community Server, failed login attempts, and other related status and activity messages.

| ID | Message | Category | EventDate | ▶ EventID | EventType | SettingsID |
|----|---------|----------|-----------|-----------|-----------|------------|
| 351 | CS.Web Started | Application | 10/21/2006 9:43:24 AM | .. 200 | 0 | -1 |
| 350 | CS.Web Started | Application | 10/20/2006 3:14:39 PM | .. 200 | 0 | -1 |
| 349 | CS.Web Stopped CS.Web Stopped _shutDownMessage= _shutDownStack= | Application | 10/19/2006 6:33:54 PM | .. 201 | 0 | -1 |
| 348 | CS.Web Started | Application | 10/19/2006 2:57:28 PM | .. 200 | 0 | -1 |
| 347 | Comment (113): re: Community Server - A User Guide was deleted by 2100 | Weblogs | 10/19/2006 10:13:27 AM | .. 444 | 1 | 1000 |
| 346 | CS.Web Started | Application | 10/19/2006 10:08:42 AM | .. 200 | 0 | -1 |
| 345 | CS.Web Started | Application | 10/19/2006 9:40:01 AM | .. 200 | 0 | -1 |
| 344 | CS.Web Stopped CS.Web Stopped _shutDownMessage= _shutDownStack= | Application | 10/18/2006 5:45:23 PM | .. 201 | 0 | -1 |
| 343 | CS.Web Started | Application | 10/18/2006 3:37:17 PM | .. 200 | 0 | -1 |
| 342 | CS.Web Started | Application | 10/18/2006 11:01:19 AM | .. 200 | 0 | -1 |

As you can see from the above screenshot, the grid displays a list of events that occurred during the usage of Community Server. You can view the details of each event in the **Event Log Entry** pop-up window when you click the relevant link that in the **ID** column

In a same way, you can view the log of each event separately. The log will be separated into pages if there are numerous entries.

# Summary

In this chapter, we have examined the management of some of the core aspects involved with the usage of Community Server. You have learned how to implement Google AdSense and Amazon's affiliate system into Community Server. You have learned about the working of censorship, spam and IP address blocker, and the management of licenses. You also learned about the Member Points system and the creation and management of URL Redirects.

# Deploying Community Server

We hope that you have now gained sufficient knowledge to work effectively with Community Server. We examined the process of deploying it on a local system in Chapter 2. Your next task is to properly deploy Community Server on a web-hosting server and this appendix describes the steps required to get your site hosted on a live web server.

## Registering a Domain Name

A domain name is your identity on the web. Hence, you need to pick up a name that resembles your business. You can register a domain name from a provider of your choice. Two of the popular providers of domain name registrations are NetworkSolutions (`http://www.netsol.com`) and Go Daddy (`http://www.godaddy.com`).

## Obtaining a Web Space

Once you register a domain name, you need to obtain server space from a web hosting provider. Initially, a minimum amount of space such as 100 MB is sufficient. You can upgrade it later on depending upon the usage of your site. You should make sure that the web server contains the following software:

1. Windows Server 2003
2. ASP.NET 1.1 or ASP.NET 2.0
3. Microsoft SQL Server 2000 or Microsoft SQL Server 2005

Moreover, you should ask your provider questions regarding monthly bandwidth, location of the server, future upgrade capability of your web space, etc.

You can also post general hosting-related questions at:
`http://forums.asp.net/default.aspx?GroupID=29`

# Uploading Files

Before proceeding to upload the files, you should first create the required database. Refer to Chapter 2 for more information regarding creation of databases.

Normally, all hosting packages include a web-based Control Panel for managing your website. Helm (`http://www.webhostautomation.com`) is one of the fastest Control Panels for Windows Servers followed by Plesk (`http://www.swsoft.com`). Both of these hosting Control Panels provide a facility to install Community Server from within the web-based system without any need for you to either run the built-in installer or upload the files to the server using File Transfer Protocol (FTP). All the required files will be automatically placed into the appropriate folder on the server upon successful completion of the setup process.

Many popular web hosting providers such as ASPnix (`http://www.aspnix.com`) and HostingFest (`http://www.hostingfest.com`) provide technical support for configuration and installation of Community Server for your website.

You can, however, install only the version of Community Server provided by your web hosting provider using the above mentioned method. If you wish to upgrade or install a newer version then you should manually upload the files by using File Transfer Protocol (FTP) software such as SmartFTP (`http://www.smartftp.com`), CuteFTP (`http://www.cuteftp.com`), or CoreFTP (`http://www.coreftp.com/`).

You can also install Community Server on a Virtual Private Server (VPS) offered by popular companies such as ASPnix (`http://www.aspnix.com`). The advantage of hosting the site on a VPS is that you get access to the remote server so that you can directly download and unzip the files from within the remote desktop without any need to contact your web hosting provider.

The main disadvantage of uploading the files using FTP is that it will take a substantial amount of time to upload the files inside certain folders. We would suggest you to upload the required ZIP file inside the root directory of your website and contact your provider to unzip them in order to avoid the difficulty. You should then run the built-in installer to set up Community Server on your site as described in Chapter 2.

You have successfully deployed Community Server on a live web server. You can now sit back and relax while the visitors browse your site. You have already seen the powerful management capabilities of Community Server in the earlier chapters of this book. You need to use all the available techniques effectively to maximize the efficiency of your website. You should also make use of Search Engine Optimization (SEO) to effectively market and thereby boost the traffic of your website (`http://en.wikipedia.org/wiki/Search_engine_optimization`).

# Index

moderator 107
moving 113-115
navigating 106
popular posts, managing 121
post/page, general settings 119
replying to 99
replying to with quote 99, 100
sorting 106
threads/page, general settings 119
threads versus posts 106

**post settings**
allow comments on my blog 73
allow readers to rate posts 74
allow tracking of external references to my
    posts (trackbacks) 74
anonymous posting, enabling 229
auto name posts 74
comment moderation 73
emoticons, allowing 229
forum rating type 230
managing 229, 230
new posts are displayed on my blog's
    homepage 74
new posts are displayed on this site's
    homepage 74
number of top posters 230
post censorship, enabling 229
publish post excerpts when my content is
    syndicated (RSS) 74
results/page, searching 230
send me email notification 73
user posting performance 230
user rank as a picture, displaying 230

# R

**ranks**
about 121
creating 121
viewing 122
**reader**
about 177
permissions for users, granting 182
RSS feed, adding 178
RSS feed, aggregating 179, 180
RSS feed, managing 181, 182
working with 178

**reader and roller**
about 12
content mirroring 13, 178
example 177
last modified interval, settings 185
overview 177
page size, settings 186
reader 12, 178
roller 13, 15, 183
RSS feeds 12
RSS result size, settings 186
settings 185
truncation length, settings 185
**Really simple syndication feeds.** *See* **RSS
    feeds**
**registration settings**
account activation 202
allow banned users to login 200
allow login 200
allow new user registration 200
new user moderation level 201
password recovery 202
password regular expression pattern 202
show control checkboxes 201
username maximum length 201
username minimum length 201
username regular expression pattern 201
**reports**
about 237
exception report 238, 239
exception report, filtering 239
feature availability 237
for blogs 241, 242
for forums 242, 243
for sites 240, 241
in Community Server 240
jobs report 239, 240
**roller**
aggregate in assigned blog, settings 184
aggregate in site blog roll, settings 184
content mirroring 178, 183
excerpt size, settings 184
post full text, settings 184
posts, viewing 184, 185
pull interval, settings 184
settings 184
working with 183

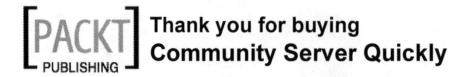

**Thank you for buying**
**Community Server Quickly**

## About Packt Publishing

Packt, pronounced 'packed', published its first book "*Mastering phpMyAdmin for Effective MySQL Management*" in April 2004 and subsequently continued to specialize in publishing highly focused books on specific technologies and solutions.

Our books and publications share the experiences of your fellow IT professionals in adapting and customizing today's systems, applications, and frameworks. Our solution based books give you the knowledge and power to customize the software and technologies you're using to get the job done. Packt books are more specific and less general than the IT books you have seen in the past. Our unique business model allows us to bring you more focused information, giving you more of what you need to know, and less of what you don't.

Packt is a modern, yet unique publishing company, which focuses on producing quality, cutting-edge books for communities of developers, administrators, and newbies alike. For more information, please visit our website: www.packtpub.com.

## Writing for Packt

We welcome all inquiries from people who are interested in authoring. Book proposals should be sent to authors@packtpub.com. If your book idea is still at an early stage and you would like to discuss it first before writing a formal book proposal, contact us; one of our commissioning editors will get in touch with you.

We're not just looking for published authors; if you have strong technical skills but no writing experience, our experienced editors can help you develop a writing career, or simply get some additional reward for your expertise.

## Building Websites with VB.NET and DotNetNuke 4

ISBN: 1-904811-99-X          Paperback: 350 pages

A practical guide to creating and maintaining your own DotNetNuke website, and developing new modules and skins.

1. Create and manage your own website with DotNetNuke

2. Customize and enhance your site with skins and custom modules

3. Extensive coverage of the DAL and DAL+ for custom module development

4. Complete coverage of setup, administration, and development

## GDI+ Application Custom Controls with Visual C# 2005

ISBN: 1-904811-60-4          Paperback: 272 pages

A fast-paced example-driven tutorial to building custom controls using Visual C# 2005 Express Edition and .NET 2.0.

1. Learn about custom controls and the GDI+

2. Walks through great examples like PieChart control

3. Customize and develop your own controls

Please check **www.PacktPub.com** for information on our titles

www.ingramcontent.com/pod-product-compliance
Lightning Source LLC
Chambersburg PA
CBHW062110050326

40690CB00016B/3277

* 9 7 8 1 8 4 7 1 9 0 8 7 1 *